Ghostly Spirits
of Warren County North Carolina & Beyond

*Cynthia —
with Love & Gratitude —
Arlene S. Bice
17 June 2016*

Arlene S. Bice

OTHER BOOKS BY THE AUTHOR

Images of America –Bordentown
Images of America- New Egypt & Plumsted
Images of America – Bordentown Revisited
Post Card Series -- Bordentown

Ghosts of Bordentown
Haunted Bordentown
Life & Labyrinth – A Collection of Memoir & Poetry
Major Fraser's –A House and A History
Living with Ghosts
The Afternoon Crowd

Copyright Arlene S. Bice 2016

All rights reserved. No part of this publication may be reproduced, stored in a retrieval system, or transmitted in any form or by any means, electronic, mechanical, recording or otherwise, without the prior written permission of the author.

The accounts in this book have been researched and believed true to the best of the author's knowledge. Some of the conversations may be paraphrased but the content is what happened. The stories and photos have been given with written consent.

Printed in the United States of America.

Revised Edition 2016

True stories of haunting, ghosts and paranormal moments. 2. History in Warren County, North Carolina. 3. American history.

Cover Photo by Aaron Bukowski

Photos by Aaron Bukowski

ACKNOWLEDGEMENTS

Many thanks are offered in great appreciation for the help in obtaining background, facts, and information for the stories herein. These thanks go to all who have given up their experiences freely so others may enjoy and learn from them.

TABLE OF CONTENTS

INTRODUCTION..1

PART ONE: WARREN COUNTY 3

Ridgeway

Happenings at Oakley Hall Plantation 3

No Rest at Traveler's Rest: Lucy Holtzmann's Story 12

Unrest at Traveler's Rest: Don & Ernie's Story 14

A Mother Waits: The Babs Holtzman Story 18

Warrenton

Playful Family in Blount Cottage: Robert's Story 23

Imprints and Footfalls: The Kathleen Derring-Shingler Story 27

Battle Between Good and Evil: Shirley's Story................39

A Mayor Returns: W.A. Miles Hardware Store................42

Wise

Restoration Kicks up the Ghosts: Todd's Story 47

Johnny Reb, Indians and More: Nancy's Story................59

Warren Plains

Children's Tea Party: The Putnam Story 63

Interview with a Ghost Hunter: Michael La Chiana of THHS 75

PART TWO: LEGENDS 83

Secrets in Person's Ordinary 83

A Soldier's Impressions: The Braxton Bragg Story 90

PART THREE: TALES BROUGHT TO LAKE GASTON 95

People and Their Ghosts: The Ann Herbert Stories 96

Spirit Doesn't Know She is Dead: Heidi's Story 103

The Hobo and the Depression: Lynne's Stories 109

The Strange Visits of William King By Barbara H. Hobbs 119

SOURCES 122

INTRODUCTION

It seems that genetics play a role in some people being more psychically developed than others, even though that gene hasn't been found yet. You will note in some of the stories here, the teller will mention that their mother or grandmother had a definite sixth sense. Often children will display psychic phenomena, but either leave it behind in their childhood or learn to hide it because of criticism from people saying "Don't be silly. You're making that up." When a child hears that often enough, she is likely to hide her experiences or deny them.

Carl Jung spoke of psychic fields. Sedona, which is a highly charged area for psychic phenomena, has its red rocks, we, in this area of north central North Carolina have red clay on top of granite which contains about 10% quartz. I believe this area is charged to receive psychic phenomena, too. Creativity seems to respond to the same geological make-up, especially when you add water; here that would be the lakes and rivers.

Paranormal researchers obtain much from the Civil War battlefields of Antietam and Gettysburg which sit on granite/quartz geologic underground. Vicksburg, Mississippi reportedly doesn't have the same number of ghostly sightings although it has the same horrors of war. It doesn't have the granite/quartz underground either.

I am not a ghost hunter. Nor do I claim to be an expert or a medium or highly sensitive to the paranormal activities of others. I have had *visits* from the other side of the veil, both directly and through a medium. For me, they've been ultimately enlightening experiences. Also for me, it reconfirms the Christian, Hindu, and Buddhist belief that there is life after life.

Although I have long been interested in paranormal phenomena, my seeking truth and knowledge on life-after-life comes from personal events in my life. Perhaps this is because most of my ancestors and two of my children have *passed over* without reaching an elderly age.

In 1986 my mother passed away at the age of 72, the longest life of any of my antecedents. She never *came* to me but she told me of *visits* she had before she died. More than once and at different times her mother and her best friend Annie had *come* to her to tell her they would help to make her *crossing-over* easier. (Her words.) She died very peacefully. It showed on her face. She was sitting in her favorite living room chair when I came in to check on her after work. I thought she was asleep.

My brother Albert experienced the same *visits* in the last year of his life, but it was our mother, our 'Aunt' Edie, and our neighbor Kip Stencil, who came to him. She was his favorite person when he was growing up, especially as a teenager,

I've read a bit of Albert Einstein's theory on how he understood time. To his thinking, the future already exists in a time-space continuum with a third element connecting the two dimensionally even though the average person can't see it. The world exists also, even though we can't see England while looking through our window, we know it's there.

PART ONE: WARREN COUNTY

Oakley Hall Plantation   Photo by Aaron Bukowski

Ridgeway

Happenings at Oakley Hall Plantation
Don and Ernie each spoke, sometimes one starting and the other filling in facts and details.

They have restored other homes before moving to Warren County. Since they had the experience, both thought it would be a good idea to find another house to restore as they planned their early retirement from their respective careers. Reading the National Trust Preservation magazine with this intention brought their eyes to a Preservation North Carolina property; Oakley Hall. The former plantation manor in Ridgeway sounded worth a weekend trip to investigate.

Local preservationist Richard Hunter met them at the house that had protective plywood over all the windows. By flashlight they fell in love with the open staircase interior, huge high-ceilinged rooms, and the Italianate architecture. They topped off the visit with lunch in nearby Warrenton, the county seat. Seeing the town convinced them. This was the place they wanted to live.

Don and Ernie were so impressed with Warrenton that they also bought commercial buildings on Main Street. In one they opened up Oakley Hall Antiques which Don's mother, Dot staffs. Then they purchased a cottage nearby for her. They remain involved in the community's activities and associations donating time, money and skills.

The interview begins when I'm settled into the 6,000 square foot Oakley Hall Plantation House with owners and restorers Don Arnold and Ernie Fleming. We're sitting in the front room left of the entrance doors.

Don begins: We bought the plantation in 1991 taking several months to negotiate the purchase of fifteen acres of land along with the house. The house was ominous; all closed up and had been vacant for at least fifteen years. Plaster was all over the place; we were told a teenager had tried to burn it down. He set a fire in every room on the ground floor.

It was a tough job to get started in restoring it. Friends thought we were crazy. But we were so excited. We visualized what it could be.

We could barely wait to begin. Our first night sleeping here was *six years* after our purchase.

At first we pulled a 40-foot trailer out back and stayed there on weekends. In 1993 we bought the Marshall-Moore House (aka Travelers' Rest) to live in until Oakley Hall was completed.

I have slept many nights in Oakley Hall alone. I feel warm and comfortable here. Every house we've ever owned was haunted. At Spring House where we lived in High Point (North Carolina) we'd be having a dinner party and our guests would see Mrs. Pearson cleaning. They'd be frightened by her and we'd be saying, 'Oh, don't worry she won't harm you. But, tell us what she looks like! What's she wearing tonight? We know she's here but we've never seen her.'

That's been our experiences in both these houses. We glean other peoples' reactions and hear their stories but not actually seen anything ourselves. We ask them exactly what they saw and how do they feel about it.

We always thought that our intentions in restoring the beauty and integrity of these homes were so noble that the former residents, or spirits, respected our presence and didn't bother us. I think that's consistently true. We always give so much credit to the history of these spirits who were once people. We tell of their lives so they'll be honored and remembered as such. We're a connection to their existence and continuance. Why would they make us want to run away?

Renowned architect Jacob Holt built the Plantation House for Dr. William J. Hawkins in 1855. He moved into it with his second wife, Lucy Norfleet Clark, sister of his deceased first wife Mary Alethea (also spelled Althea) Clark. He and Mary Alethea lived in the 1845 cottage that sits to the rear of Oakley Hall.

Earlier members of the Hawkins family served in public life, owned thousands of plantation acres, fought in the Revolutionary War, were part of the Provincial Congress, and were lawyers and governors.

They've also held positions as Indian agents, senators, doctors, bankers, and railroad owners.

The Hawkins family was one of the founding families of the University of North Carolina. A member of the family sat on that Board until the late 1800s. There is an excess of 14,000 documents in the Southern Collection in Chapel Hill on the Hawkins family.

In time Dr. William Joseph Hawkins was drawn to Raleigh to pursue interests in the Raleigh-Gaston Railroad and later banking. Son Marmaduke purchased Oakley Hall from his father.

Marmaduke Hawkins

Marmaduke Hawkins graduated the University of Virginia; was an attorney in partnership with Governor Thomas Walter Bickett; State Senator; plantation owner. He was the country gentleman and became head of the County Commissioners. The front room (where we sat) was the focal point of local government for a long time. It was also the Gentlemen's Parlour. Many important decisions were made in this room.

Don continues: The room was also used for laying out the caskets of family members who passed on. In those days funeral parlors were not used in this area. The casket would be carried out the front doors and loaded onto the train that stopped at the entrance to the property and taken to Raleigh.

Ernie fills in: We came up every Friday night in February 1993 to pay the workers for their week of work on projects we assigned to them. At that time we were doing an addition on the back of the house. It was a snowy weekend; the guys had worked all week inside doing the upstairs pink bedroom. That room was one of the most ominous of all. It had plaster piled on the floor; it was a mess.

The guys said they wanted to talk to us because they were concerned about something that happened to them. These two guys never drank on the job, they were dependable, every day type of guys, very reliable people. They smoked cigarettes but did not drink until after the workday ended.

They started with "Has anything unusual ever happened to you guys in the house? I ask because something happened to us this week."

"Well we heard the house has some . . . . stories. What happened?" Don said.

"While we were upstairs working a man walked out of the wall and crossed the bedroom, never acknowledging us, and walked into the wall across the room."

Don picked up the conversation from there: They told me that they individually saw it, clearly, looked at each other and said in unison, "Did you see that, too?" They both nodded that they had, were discussing it briefly when the man came back through the wall, again crossed the room and re-entered the wall he first came from. At that point they left stating that they needed to have a cigarette.

They went outside, talked it over and decided whether they should go back in to work. Nothing like that had ever happened to either one of them.

It seems the intense spirit of Marmaduke Hawkins is still here.

The house at the time wasn't much more than a shell but we were promoting Warren County so we were organizing bus tours. Even friends came out of curiosity from as far away as High Point.

One lady clairvoyant came on a particular trip. A fair number of people had paused in front of her at the bottom of the stairs leading to the second floor. They refused to go up without really saying why. The general comment was, 'it feels like something is up there.' On these tours a variety of people came, so we just said, well, okay. What else can one say?

The clairvoyant was at the end of the group. She went upstairs to the front bedroom, the green bedroom, by herself. She said she walked into the room where she saw a man come out of the room. He clutched his breast and fell over to the floor. She could see he was trying to get back to his bed. He died in front of her. She literally backed out of the room and got back on the bus, not saying a word to anybody. A month later she contacted us and told us what she experienced. It was very convincing. She'd had experiences in the past. She further added that something was definitely going on in the house.

Marmaduke's presence is heavy and mournful in this house. His was an interesting life. His mother died shortly after Marmaduke was born in the cottage that now stands behind the plantation house. Complications of childbirth factored. After his mother passed away he and his brother Colin were sent to live with Weldon Nathaniel Edwards, cousin to Dr. William J. Hawkins. Weldon Edwards was a very powerful influential man politically, financially and socially. He had been President of the North Carolina Secession Convention. The Edwards family lived about six miles away at Poplar Mount. Mary Alethea (Marmaduke's mother) was buried there.

Weldon Edwards and his wife Mary Norfleet Edwards never had children. She felt toward Marmaduke as if he was her own child. Her husband passed away before she did, leaving the estate responsibilities in her hands and all decisions left to her. As a result she bequeathed a huge amount to Marmaduke. He also inherited from his father's estate.

It is believed that Marmaduke committed suicide here in 1920, possibly upstairs in the green bedroom. Despair at being completely over-drawn financially with no way to rectify the situation was probably a factor. He was a man of great power, deeply involved in business, relied on heavily by others, and carried a tremendous amount of responsibilities. He inherited wealth and spent all of it in his lifetime. After his death, his wife was forced to sell the plantation house to pay off his debts.

Janet Hawkins

Ernie picked up the story: When we purchased the property we just thought we were buying a big, ole house in the middle of the woods because it was all grown up around us. After it became ours a large manila envelope arrived in the mail. It was at least an inch thick. It held the information history of Oakley Hall! We then realized the place had belonged to one of the premier families of North Carolina.

Included in the envelope were photos of the exterior in various eras. We also learned there are stereoscopes of the interior of Oakley Hall that were produced for the family. We've never seen them, but maybe someday……..

The family has spread out to other areas of the country.

Years later a Hawkins' descendant stopped in our shop (Oakley Hall Antiques in Warrenton) and showed us a picture. I can hardly believe that we didn't ask for a copy. But we didn't. She had taken the picture before digital cameras were around, in the pink bedroom where the man was seen walking through the wall. There was a Victorian-dressed little girl hovering over the dresser. It was a very human-like image. The same little girl was in the picture taken in the first known picture of this house, taken in the 1870s. We believe it was Janet Hawkins. When we mention it to folks around here, they're not surprised. Everyone seems to know about the *other occupants* in our house.

Many weddings took place here and many babies were born in this house. It was quite usual for the expectant mothers in the family to go 'home' to birth their children.

Marmaduke and Rebecca's children were no exception. Daughter Janet married Milo Miletus Pendleton of the prominent Pendleton family of Raleigh and Warren County in 1906. He graduated the School of Pharmacy, University of North Carolina and was a pharmacist in Warrenton. She came to bear her second child, a daughter Katherine Clark Pendleton after their first daughter passed away less than a year old. Then she came to bear her third child. Complications set in, Milo was sent for but struggling to give birth, Janet and her baby both died before he arrived. It was the 23 February 1911. It is said that the next day, extremely distraught, Milo went into the room and fatally shot himself.

Milo's sister 'Kate' married the wealthy, influential Peter Arrington in 1907. They adopted Janet and Milo's only remaining daughter and Kate's namesake. They raised her as their own, eventually sending Katherine to the best schools in Europe. The Arrington acquaintances included King George VI and Queen Elizabeth of Great Britain.

Ms. Katherine Pendleton-Arrington grew up to be named one of the ten most beautiful women in America in the 1930s. As first President of the North Carolina State Art Society she was responsible for collecting art from all over the world and starting the North Carolina Art Museum in Raleigh. This became the first publicly supported art museum in the United States.

Rebecca Hawkins

Don continued: Another ghost we're sure is residing here is Rebecca, the wife of Marmaduke. In all the years that she lived here she was known to go to the front porch every night. She was there in all kinds of weather and is there in all kinds of weather now. Her presence is definitely there. I have never felt alone sitting and rocking on the front porch. I think she probably went to the front porch for solitude and peace away from Marmaduke's constant activity in the house. He was involved in everything and always on the move.

Traveler's Rest. Photo by Aaron Bukowski

No Rest at Traveler's Rest: Lucy Holtzmann's Story

I met Lucy Holtzmann through a mutual friend. She invited me to her home so she could tell me about the Traveler's Rest hauntings. She began with some background on the historic property.

Lucy begins: The property here in Ridgeway came to be called Travelers' Rest ca. 1750, then became known as Marshall's Tavern; in 1788 it was called Paschall's Ordinary; from 1840 – 1851 folks referred to it as Captain Daly's; the next time period 1851 – 1872 it was named Dr. T. P. Jerman's; then from 1872 – 1875 the Ridgeway Company owned it; next in 1875 – 1888 the partners of B. D. Moore and F. H. Cheatham owned it; then Cheatham left and for a long stretch of years from 1888 – 1960 the B. D. Moore family took ownership; I remember the years of 1960 – 1968 when Grace Wycoff Puryear bought it; the years after the sisters passed away from 1968 – 1993 Carl and Lee Puryear possessed it and in December of 1993 to the present Dr. Don G. Arnold and Ernest F. Fleming III acquired the property.

The back two rooms of the house were originally a stagecoach stop. The house was put together with pegs dating it to the 1700s rather than nails that were used in later construction. The bottom room in one portion is now laid out as a kitchen. There was once a narrow staircase that wound around to the second floor where the travelers stayed.

Miss Grace Puryear and her sister Miss Alice Wycoff lived there. Miss Alice had severe diabetes and her legs were removed below the knees because of it. She stayed in bed mostly.

One day Miss Alice told Miss Grace "A woman has started coming to me at night. She wears a bonnet that ties under her chin and a short fingertip cloak as travelers wore back in the 1700s and early 1800s. Under her cloak is a long full skirt that stretches to the floor. She just stands there and smiles at me, then leaves the room."

Miss Grace thought because Miss Alice was so ill her imagination was working too hard. Soon after that happened Miss Alice passed away. Then some time later Miss Grace woke up in the middle of the night and saw this same woman standing by her bed just as Miss Alice had described her. Miss Grace was a woman who wasn't afraid of anyone including the devil. In her younger years she cooked for the men at a logging camp in Maine. She wasn't about to fuss or run away.

She asked the woman, "Just what do you want?" The woman smiled at Miss Grace, left the room and went into the hall where the front door stood. Miss Grace got up and followed her. The woman turned to the right and began to descend the staircase. Then she dissolved. Poof. Gone. It was the only time she saw her as far as I know. Eventually Miss Grace passed on, too.

Later, a couple moved in with their two young daughters. After a short while the girls started telling their mother that a woman kept coming into their room at night. They described her as the same woman the Misses Alice and Grace saw. The children became so frightened that the couple only lived there a few months before they moved away.

Author's Note: Mr. Holtzmann told me of the white mule ghost. In days long past, folks would be driving the horse and buggy at night, going from here to there. All of a sudden the ghost of a white mule would appear peeking over the side of the buggy then fade away. This was usually on the Ridgeway-Drewery Road on the far side of I-85

Unrest at Traveler's Rest: Don & Ernie's Story

The same house that Lucy Holtzmann told me about has additional stories from Don and Ernie. Each spoke, sometimes one starting and the other filling in facts and details.

Don began: The Marshall-Moore House (Traveler's Rest) had been empty for a while when we bought it to stay in on weekends while we completed the restoration of Oakley Hall. We had been staying in a 40-foot trailer behind Oakley Hall until we bought Traveler's Rest. Going from a trailer to a 4,000 square foot house on four levels was liberating! Whew! The hallway is 30-foot long. I wanted to run through the house from end-to-end. We actually refer to it as 'The Inn' because it housed a number of early settlers who came here while waiting to claim their lands. And several have owned it since it was built in 1750. It's reputed to be the oldest house in Warren County and the second house in the area to have glass windows. It's also reputed to be the most haunted!

The house is in two sections; first the 'ordinary' was built for travelers who were not staying at a local plantation or home to rest while waiting for the stagecoach to arrive. The stagecoaches did not run at night. In this particular 'ordinary' prostitutes operated a brothel in one of the upstairs rooms when the stagecoach spent the night.

The house was added before 1788 when it was called Marshall's Tavern. It was referred to as the 'Devil's Den' after a lady coming to stay at Bloomsbury, Governor James Turner's plantation up the road a piece, for some unknown reason had to stay there for a night. The next morning a carriage was sent out to bring her to the plantation. She was asked at the noonday meal, "How was your trip and your accommodation at Travelers' Rest?"

"Travelers' Rest?" she replied. "It should be called the Devil's Den!"

Don and Ernie continue: We heard a lot about the ghostly activity going on at The Inn. But we saw only the results of the spirits' activity rather than seeing the actual ghosts. I spent many nights there that I was … uneasy. Of course the walls were full of snakes and bugs were plentiful. Plus there always seemed to be someone banging on the side door.

A clairvoyant student of mine came from High Point to see Oakley Hall, then came over to walk through The Inn. "You have no idea how many black snakes you have in that house!" He was indicating the Inn. "The walls are full of black snakes and the house is full of spirits!"

I knew about the snakes. I saw a five-foot long blacksnake on the kitchen counter. I eventually got rid of the mice and the snakes left automatically.

One of the spirits most often told about leaves a scent of honeysuckle in the air. Our adopted daughter, Karen spent most of one summer at the Inn with me. One afternoon she was taking a nap in her room. She was about thirty years old at the time.

She told me afterwards, "I woke up intending to rise rather than just lay there. But I couldn't. Someone or something was holding my shoulders down, gently but firmly. I was wide-awake. I didn't struggle. All of a sudden the room filled with the aroma of roses."

When she did join me in the kitchen, she said, "I think I just met one of your ghosts." She wasn't frightened at all. It was very matter-of-fact.

I'd been told that oftentimes Grace Puryear got frustrated when she lived there. She would be out visiting or shopping and come home to find the drawers of the sideboard in the hall open and her things dumped all over the floor.

We had extraordinary poltergeist activity. Our six antique goblets were in the cabinet as they should be when we left for the workweek. When we returned for the weekend, we'd find one goblet lying on its side. Not broken or knocked over, because it would have fallen to the floor and broke. It was just carefully, purposely lying down.

We each had a set of keys to the house. The extra set of keys was kept in the kitchen drawer. One Friday night when we arrived, the extra set of keys was stuck in the back door keyhole. The door was wide open. No one knew they were there in the drawer. I remember thinking that it was not a nice thing to do. Anyone could have walked into our house. Although I guess we didn't have to worry, most folks were afraid to come in anyway. No one has ever tried to tamper with the house.

Three brothers from the area agreed to paint the house for us. But one of the brothers just freaked out at the man in bib overalls that kept staring out the window at him. "There's an old farmer living in your house!' He told us when we came on the weekend. 'He's there! He is absolutely in that house!" Of course, no one was in the house that we could see.

A young couple came up to us one Sunday morning at the Inn as we were getting ready to go back to High Point for our usual workweek.

"Hi, we're visiting in the area. Years ago we used to rent this house. We just thought we would stop to see it." They said to us.

"Oh neat. What was it like?" I replied. We wanted to know about the house but they weren't about to talk about it.

They asked, "did you ever live here?"

"Sure, I've been staying here for the last year and Ernie's been here on weekends."

"Did anything unusual ever happen to you?"

"Not really." I replied although I was thinking of Karen's experience when I said it.

"This place is so haunted." Then they started telling us about their experiences. We realized the bedroom they used was the room where Karen had her 'happening'.

"The spirits were really interrupting our sleep. They moved around the room all night and they kept opening the door up. We finally wedged the door closed."

That was kind of a feeble attempt to keep the spirit out, I thought. They continued on.

"It was a winter night and there was a rumble at the door. Whatever it was pushed the door open with the wedge in it. At that point we decided we really had to move."

I replied that my mother has slept in that room many times and has never seen anything out of the ordinary. I have never actually seen anything either. Nothing. Nothing. Nothing. The snakes scared me more than anything else.

The Collins' Place   Photo by Aaron Bukowski

A Mother Waits: The Babs Holtzman Story

I drove onto the Holtzman farm property following the dirt road snaking through trees and shrubbery into a small round-about behind the big white farmhouse. As I came to a stop, a couple of big dogs greeted my Chevy Tracker with barks alerting the family that a stranger had come calling. I waited patiently too wary to step out of the car until someone showed up to escort me. The dogs look friendly. Their tails were wagging, but why take a chance.

Mr. Holtzman stepped out of the enclosed porch door heading my way. I grinned, feeling welcome already. A bubbly Babs and Reuben Holtzman have been living in their house for 34 years when I spoke to her about the 'happenings' in their house. Babs did the talking.

She began: In the earlier years of our marriage, my husband was a trouble-shooter for the company he worked for, resulting in our having to move from time to time. We came to Ridgeway while he was still working for the company. He was born and raised here and came from a farming family. He told me that if he ever left his company he wanted to come back to farming again.

During that brief visit we were driving down a country road and I saw this house. It was obviously old and badly in need of repair. I said rather casually but pointing my finger, "If we ever come this way again, I want to live in that house."

It took a few years but my husband decided he did want to do farming instead of roaming around from place to place so here we are. He wanted to build me a new house pointing out to me the sags in the old farmhouse. But I could see the charm that could be uncovered in this old place. I didn't mind sags, having a few of my own. The house is over 150 years old. It was beginning to fall apart and it called out to me. I saw the character of the house. We called in an architect. He checked it out.

"It's a sound house; solid," he told us.

As soon as we moved in, one of the first things I did was put a candle in the upstairs front window. Reuben said, "Now why did you do that?"

"I want folks to know that even though the front porch is falling apart, they are welcome in our home." It took us some time but we lovingly restored the house to how it should be. A bit of time passed and we began to notice a few odd 'happenings.'

It first began when my husband clearly heard footsteps upstairs when we were downstairs. This happened repeatedly. He would run up but could never catch anyone there. My children often told me, "Mama, there's a woman upstairs." I just thought, 'kids, you know.'

Then one night I woke from a deep sleep to feel breathing on my cheek. I opened my eyes, nothing was there but I could feel it! There could be no other explanation for it.

Soon after my son turned eighteen, a young man's age, he called out to me from his twin bed in the back room.

"Mama, come help me! Mama, come quick!" I went running, scared to death. When I entered the room I felt the coldness right away. Ice cold. Not like the weather-cold and completely different from the air in the hallway.

"What's wrong? What's wrong?" I was calling out.

"She won't let me up! She's holding me down! She's keeping me here."

Something or someone was pinning his shoulders to the bed. Finally he was released. "Stay, Mama. Stay." I sat for a while just to reassure him.

My husband has seen the ghost and my children have seen her. I've never seen her, only felt her breathing on me that one particular night.

Old-timer Zeb St. Sing lived around here. Zeb could *see* things. He often told me he *saw* spirits sitting on my front porch when he rode by. He also saw a woman in the same front window where I placed my lighted candle.

Strangely enough, when I sent a photo of our new 'old' home to my sister (she's a contractor and builds new, modern homes) she called me on the phone. Laughingly she told me "Who's the ghost in the front window?" I thought she was joking. She sent me a copy of the photo and sure enough a ghost is in the same window where I put my lighted candle. Just like Zeb St. Sing told me.

In 1848 a Randolph Macon College subsidiary school was started on this site. Their house was the dormitory for the students. When the school burned down, the students left. The Captain, referring to his

Civil War ranking, along with his wife Mollie, nee Mary W. Plummer, moved into the house.

They had six children: Mary, known as 'Asia' was the only one who married. After her husband passed away she moved back into the family home. Also there was Lucy, Annie, Thomas, Rebecca, and Johnston called Pettigrew. Rebecca arranged to have the family cemetery enclosed at Pleasant Hill and a stone engraved for each member. Pleasant Hill was the large plantation nearby owned by the Captain's father and where Benjamin grew up.

A Rev. Gerald Collins from Black Mountain (North Carolina) stopped in to visit. I was telling him that I thought the house was haunted. He asked, "Do you know the story of the house?" Since I didn't, he began to tell me:

"A matter of disagreement developed between Colonel Collins and his son. The Colonel kicked him out of the house. The boy's mother never got over it. Her sadness at the loss of her son in the home stayed with her. She immediately put a candle in the upstairs window to let her son know she was thinking of him and he was welcome to come back home."

Babs nodded: I found out that it was the same window I unknowingly put my candle in as a sign of welcome. She knew he passed by on the train everyday as he headed for Richmond to conduct business there. As the train tracks were located across the roadway, she also knew he was able to see the window with the candle flickering in the window, sending him the message.

He never came. Years passed slowly while she mourned for her son. She never knew what happened to him or where he went or what he was doing. Then one fateful day in 1947 she received money from the military as a death benefit. Now she knew he would never again see the candle in the window nor would he ever return to her.

Author's Notes: Through modern research I found that Johnston Pettigrew Collins put business aside and joined the army. He was stationed at Fort Whipple in Prescott, Arizona in 1910. This was a time before Arizona became the 48th state (in 1912) and they were still setting up Indian Reservations. Mexico was attacking and waging battles along the Arizona and New Mexico borders. Pettigrew was a part of this action in the still-wild west. He was there when Arizona gave the vote to women nine years before the federal government granted women the right to vote.

In 1920 Pettigrew was still in the army stationed in Watertown, Massachusetts. He probably fought in World War I. By this time his father had passed away but he may not have known that.

He left instructions for his body to be shipped home to North Carolina to be buried in the family cemetery in Warren County. The same cemetery Rebecca had enclosed. His wishes were carried out.

Warrenton

Playful Family in Blount Cottage: Robert's Story

Robert moved into one of the early houses of Warrenton that had at one time evolved into a hotel. His living room served as the lobby.

Shortly after moving into the house he was talking to his long-time friend Elaine by telephone. They have retained a close friendship since high school days. She happens to be psychically developed.

"You have an older gentleman, his daughter and a young gentleman who comes to visit her, living in your house." She told him matter-of-factly.

He was stunned.

"Furthermore, this week they will play with your electric and knock your books off your shelf."

He laughed not quite taking her comment seriously. Five days later as he was preparing to bed down for the night, the lights went off in his house. He knew without checking that his electric bill was paid-up and a new bill not due for another three weeks. Looking out of the window he could see Main Street had lights, his neighbor Elsie's lights were streaming out of her windows, and the Hardware Café window lights seemed to be boasting that there was nothing wrong at that location.

He said "Oh, well" to himself and climbed into bed. The next morning when he got up to face the day everything electrical in his house worked as it was meant to be working.

But the following night as he was dozing off to sleep a loud 'clump, clump, clump' made him sit up in bed alerting all his senses. "What's that?" he said out loud to no one listening. At least to no one he could see was listening. Straining for further noises but not really wanting to hear anything else, he slid under the covers wishing for sleep to come immediately.

In the morning he found his array of framed photos spread out face down. They had been placed at various angles so if one fell over, it wouldn't affect the others. So what happened? Books had tumbled off his shelves and lay on the floor. In a near panic he called Elaine.

"Calm down," she told him. "Just tell them in a firm voice to leave you alone."

He did just that. Standing at the base of his stairs so his voice would carry throughout the entire house, he shouted in his best 'don't mess with me' tone, "Leave me alone!" They did, for some time anyway.

Time passed. One day as he was working on the computer in his home office, sitting near his personal heater, he glanced over as he felt increasingly warmer and warmer and warmer. The heater was set at an appropriate temperature but the temperature was rising and rising and rising. This reliable heater that he had been using for the last few years was behaving unnaturally. He readjusted the setting, went back to writing on his computer determined to ignore this little interruption. Before long the air in his office got warmer and warmer and warmer.

"Stop this!" he bellowed. They did. The heater returned to normal and to Robert's satisfaction life went back to a normal state.

The Blount Family

Author's Note: Warrenton before the War Between the States was the wealthiest community in the state. It boasted of culture, recreation and also carried a highly prized reputation for its schools culminating a century of private schooling for both boys and girls. Even then it was a choice place to live.

Many people moved here or built a town house as a secondary home away from the plantation, partly because of summer diseases that took the lives of young children in the flat low country of the coastal area. They also wanted the social aspect of being in town to see friends outside the family while attending dances, soirees and a chance to participate in the political discussions for the gents.

Thomas Augustus and Frances Louisa Clark Blount came from their Washington, Beaufort County home prior to 1850 for the education of their children. Son James was born in 1842 followed by Sarah also called Sallie, Louisa also called Laura, Thomas, Fannie, and Mary.

Both Thomas and Frances carried a long line of heritage in North Carolina. Ancestors James and Claire Blount traveled from Astley Parish, Worcestershire, England to the Albemarle Chowan County area in the early 1600s. Frances Louisa Clark's mother was also a Blount.

All went smoothly until 1854 when the congregation charged one of their members, Mr. Blount, to engage Jacob Holt to augment and expand the Emmanuel Episcopal Church. Thomas Bragg built the original, plain oblong sanctuary in the mid 1820s. The congregation had grown in size and wealth and disdained the plainness of the wooden church. They desired a roomier structure.

Blount took on the responsibility as requested and contracted the builder to undertake the improvements. Holt complied by enlarging the building overall and turning the appearance into a Victorian Romanesque Revival style adding a much desired steeple. Problems arose when Holt didn't complete the project in the time frame the Emmanuel leadership demanded. Furthermore the costs had risen and both sides had trouble coming to agreeable financial terms. A few of the parishioners held Mr. Blount accountable and lay blame and anger on him. The project was finally completed and satisfied to all parties by January 1858.

The Blount family returned to Washington City by 1860 possibly because of the air of distraught left from the accusations of his fellow parishioners. But the Cottage still carries his name. It may also still carry the imprints of the young adults of the family receiving social callers in happier times. They may have retained their mischievous nature and now add inquisitive habits about new objects in a modern age.

The father Thomas passed away in 1861. The oldest son James enlisted in the Confederacy as a Sergeant. Frances Louisa and all the children survived the War.

Somerville-Graham House   Photo by Aaron Bukowski

Imprints and Footfalls:
The Kathleen Derring-Shingler Story

Kathleen gave me a tour of the Somerville-Graham House filling me in on her experiences along the way. Her psychic abilities are somewhat developed as were her mother's. "Sometimes it just pops up" she tells me, but she cannot call on that talent all the time. This phenomenon came to her attention when she was eleven years old. She's also owned old farmhouses, has refurbished them and has been an antique dealer for a number of years. Her husband Bob and she knew this house would be a challenge to restore. They were ready to jump into the work and breathe life back into this ca. 1850 Jacob Holt-built antebellum house. Long before they moved in, Kathleen drew the floor plans, placing furniture on paper exactly where she 'knew' it belonged.

Bob and Kathleen were still living in Florida after they bought the house, taking trips up every 2 ½ months to check on the house and do some work, some transporting of furniture, etc. In the meantime her stepson Justin was here doing some painting.

Kathleen begins her story: In late October Justin was busy painting the front room. He was content doing his work in the big, empty house. While he was painting near the windows, he glanced outside and noticed the trees were a brilliant orange. The trees were so stunning in beauty that he took a photograph. That's when Justin saw the *form of a man* watching him; an apparition. It was not threatening, it was just watching him. He left the photo in the house to show to us. It disappeared. It's gone. No one else was in the house but the photo is gone. We have not been able to find it since.

When he was painting the walls in another front room, downstairs, an argument started up between him and his girlfriend Jennie. They're young and tend to argue about a lot of things. Bob and I were in Florida at the time. But we got the phone call. During the argument, the big, front dormer window blew----out! The whole window! It didn't blow in from an outside source; it blew out from inside the house! Nothing touched it! It just blew out! Jennie told me later that my cat took off running just before it happened! He must have seen something the two of them didn't see.

This was during a cold February. I called a guy to come replace the window immediately. I hated to see all our heat flying out the open window. The guy was amazed because he had been thinking that a bird may have flown into the window, but the window would have fallen in, not out, he told us.

Justin and Jennie noticed items flying off the table while they were arguing. I reminded him to have his arguments outside. It was too expensive to have them inside the house. Obviously our house ghosts don't like dissension. Jennie jokingly commented to me that she must be getting Helen upset.

Author Note: Helen Reid Franklin was the last person who lived in the house before Kathleen and Bob bought it in 2005. Although born in Anderson, South Carolina she spent her youth and childhood first in Littleton then Warrenton. East Carolina's Teacher's College came after graduating from the John Graham High School. A short time was spent teaching kindergarten children before she moved to Athens, Georgia to work in the office of Belk department store. That's where she met her future husband, the newly enlisted Army man, George Walton Franklin. They married in 1942 and spent thirty years traveling the world with the military. Serving as president of the Officers' Wives Club was only one of the many services she gladly offered between volunteering at the base hospitals, thrift shops and chapel nurseries.

Always feeling that home was Warrenton, she returned in 1972 but it wasn't until 1979 that she bought the historic Somerville-Graham House. Opening her home, which she filled to overflowing with wonderful old antiques and flowers, to architecture students and professors was a pleasure to her. Historic Home Tours, Little Garden Club, United Daughters of the Confederacy and other meetings were welcomed to her home with the same southern charm and hospitality reminiscent of its first mistress, Matilda Somerville.

Her inclination for volunteering continued in Warrenton where she delivered a hot meal and a little companionship for the Meals-On-Wheels program. People who knew Helen said she radiated sunshine, she just loved her home, and she loved flowers. She was in her late 90s when she left the house to live in the Warren Hills Home.

Kathleen filled me in on more recent information. Her respect for Helen is obvious, so is the joy and love of the house that Helen reportedly felt. "I understand that after she moved into the retirement home the place was sold under a land contract, but I heard that it was too much work and the people left. I wonder if they saw things that disquieted them.

She continued: It then sat vacant for a year before we came along. We had been searching in North Carolina for a house. This was the very last house we looked at and we had looked at a lot of houses.

I wanted to go visit Helen after we signed the sale papers prior to unpacking our things. Then I learned that she *passed away* after we bought the place and before we even unpacked. I feel like she knew her home was going to be loved and cared for like she wanted.

We walked into the dining room where Kathleen pointed to the table: This is where the first unsettling thing happened as we were moving in; we had a kitchen table here in the dining room where we placed CDs all across the top of it. We were just unpacking boxes when the CDs went flying off the table onto the floor. It was as if someone stretched out an arm and scooped them all away! We just stood there, looking at each other, wondering what was going on here. The table was perfectly level, not unbalanced. After a few minutes of being stunned and not having a clue to what just happened, we continued unpacking, I was thinking that I would deal with that later. We had to get the U-Haul truck back to the rental office. Logic and the expense factor weighed in.

As we wandered into the large front to back foyer, Kathleen expanded on the unexplained happenings going on: A bit later Bob came down from the attic saying he had found some pictures. That's great, I told him. We'll hang them somewhere. It'll be neat to have something up that is part of the house's history. I walked into this open foyer under the front stairway to show him where it should go.

Later Bob filled the air mattress in the passageway that we planned to sleep on until we set up beds the next day. It was a hot day that we knew would turn into a hot night so we put the fan in there to get the air circulating. As soon as we stretched out on the airbed, it blew up! We found ourselves flat on the floor, stunned! Then I don't know why, but I looked up and saw the painting gone from the wall.

I suddenly asked him why he took the painting of the woman down. He told me, "I didn't have any picture of a woman. I'll show you the picture I found." With that said; he took me into the other room and showed me the picture of Renoir's 'Girl with a Watering Can.' "This is the picture I found," he told me.

Kathleen looked at me expressively: I know I saw the woman's portrait on the wall. She was of the antebellum style, wearing a blue gown and had brown hair. I wondered if it was a portrait of someone in the original family. Spooky, I thought. Weird.

I've seen pictures of the Graham family but haven't found any images of any Somerville member. They were the original family here. I'll keep searching. I also remember lying flat on the floor, since the air mattress blew up, and thinking, this is like living in a museum.

Her story continued with further experiences: We hear walking upstairs all the time. It's so common that we don't pay any attention to it. Outlines of numbers are on the doors, probably left from when it was Graham High School. Boys boarded here so that may account for the volume of footsteps that we hear.

The White Christmas Tree   Photo by Aaron Bukowski

Author's Note 2: A heavenly white Christmas tree stands in the corner near the fireplace of one front bedroom. It is adorned with white angels, doves, and other ornaments all exuding the feeling of peace and joy. It is breathtaking to look at in any time of year. A life-size young girl mannequin stands next to it, as if she is in the middle of trimming the tree. She is as graceful as a sculptured work of art. The scene casts an aura on the room bringing life to it.

Kathleen: I came into this room to clean it one afternoon after guests of ours left. I was in a bit of a hurry. I rushed in, and then stopped. A vapor was right near the tree. It seemed to be hovering. Maybe it was looking it over, I don't know. It moved as if it noticed me. It turned toward me, moved again and stopped. Then it moved all the way across the room. I just stood there stunned. All of a sudden I just chuckled and said aloud, 'Helen is that you? How do you like the tree?' Then I left it to do whatever it was doing.

Period Gowns   Photo by Aaron Bukowski

We strolled across the hall into the other front bedroom as Kathleen kept on talking. She showed me a gown ca. 1850 similar to the one in the portrait that she had *seen*. The other one was a beautiful silk wedding gown made in 1831. She bought the gowns in 2007 when she and Bob played with the idea of opening the house as a Bed & Breakfast. She planned to display the period gowns on mannequins. They have since discarded the idea of the B & B wanting to just enjoy the house themselves.

The wedding gown once hung in the Smithsonian Institute. It now lay fanned across the antique bed. She picked up her thread of the story. I took note of the gown spread across the bed as it is here. (She indicated to me.) I was unpacking. The closet would hold our clothes. So I asked Bob why he laid the gown across the bed this way. He said he didn't put that dress there; that he left that stuff up to me. I just looked at him understanding that things in this house just seem to happen.

Pointing to the classic commode in the room, Kathleen said: I set the commode in a different place in this room. When I next came back into the room, it was moved. I just said, 'Helen, I guess you didn't like where I put it.' With that said, I left it there.

Our friend across the street was helping us put new slats into and moving one of our beds from this same room. He glanced at the pair of candlesticks, one was broken. He told me in an alarmed voice indicating the candlestick, that he didn't do that. Oh, I know, Helen probably did that. It's becoming a joke now. Every little thing that happens is referred to Helen.

Kathleen carried on being completely open and sharing her thoughts and episodes with me.

I don't know why but I dubbed this room the Josephine Room. Later, in doing some research I learned that Josephine was the second name of a Somerville daughter.

The second daughter of John and Matilda Somerville was also named Helen although she was affectionately called Susie.

We ambled down the elegant staircase as my mind wandered, imagining the young antebellum lasses of yesteryear floating down these same steps in ball gowns swaying with their every movement, excited with the promises that the evening would bring to them. As we reach the bottom step I notice that the front door has a huge wood bar that sets across it the way it was typical to use in the days of protecting the house from Indian attack. I wondered if this were to ward off Yankees during the War Between the States.

Kathleen said: We used to put it in place when we were returning to Florida. Then I got a call the last January before we moved in permanently saying the front door was wide open.

(Apparently, ghosts ignore things like that.) My neighbor came over to reclose it afraid someone would steal something from the house. But I know that nothing bad is going to happen here. I know it. I feel it. Kathleen stated this flatly.

I heard a lot of walking on the front porch when I've been watching TV. When I went to investigate, Bob said "It's probably a cat." I had to laugh. It's not a cat. A cat pads by softly. What I heard was walking, not stomping but probably the tread of students and I only hear it at night.

We finally chose an authentic, creamy, exterior paint color for the house. As soon as the house was completely painted electrical games began. Lights were going on and off, on and off. We took it as a sign our spirits like the improvement.

Somerville-Graham House brought to life. Photo by Aaron Bukowski

The Somerville and Graham Families

Author's Note: Records show the John and Elizabeth Matilda Kearney Somerville family as being a gracious, generally happy one. Both were born to prominent families and married in 1830. Matilda (as she was called) came from Hickory Grove, home of William Kinchen Kearney and Maria Alston. He was one of the richest planters in the county. John's parents were James and Catharine Volkes Somerville of Virginia and Granville County, North Carolina. They were also wealthy plantation owners.

John contracted Jacob Holt to build a new house in front of their old one on the property facing Front Street in 1850. Afterwards John and Matilda traveled north to Philadelphia to purchase furniture. Shortly after returning from the buying trip, John became ill and passed away leaving behind his daughters, the Misses Maria, Martha Helen, Mary, Alice, Juliet Agnes, Johanna Josephine, and son James Brehon Somerville. Their niece Rebecca Brehon also lived with them.

Matilda Somerville was known for her soft spoken words, consideration and gentleness. When General Oliver Otis Howard took up residence in her home basing his headquarters there during the Reconstruction Period, she continued her southern hospitality way. This distressed a few of the townsfolk but it was her way of handling a delicate situation.

Cousin Miss Fanny Green, daughter of Major Green living in Tennessee during the War Between the States, came through the lines to live with the Somervilles until Matilda passed away in 1867. A small private cemetery, nearly inaccessible behind the Southern States property on West Franklin Street, holds the Somerville family. Fanny later married her cousin, John and Matilda's son James Brehon Somerville in 1882.

The house remained in the Somerville family until 1876 when N.M. Norwood bought it including the extensive grounds.

Again the house changed hands when John and Frances Gideon Daniel Graham came to town to run his third school. His first school located on his farm was known as the Fork Institute. When a fire displaced him, he moved to Ridgeway where he conducted his school successfully for seven years. Again fire destroyed all he had built. Several residents encouraged him to bring his school to Warrenton. The Grahams responded to the call. Most Ridgeway students followed him.

The Grahams bought the Somerville House to use for dormitories and a dining hall. The school continued to flourish and expand as John Graham's reputation as teacher and even more important, instilling his students with the desire to learn.

"Miss Frankie" as his wife was called, managed the boarding end of the school while John was teacher and principal. She was adored by the students as much as he was admired. Five of their seven children, Amma Daniel, Flora May, Maria Daniel, Virginia Williams, and William Archibald reached adulthood, graduated college, and became teachers. Three of them stayed in Warrenton to teach in his school.

Son William Archibald later became Major in the army and is remembered to be the first American to cross the Hindenburg Line. When he returned from the war he went on to serve as superintendent of schools in Wilmington and Kinston, North Carolina.

The Somerville-Graham House seems to have cosseted young people bounding through its rooms overcoming any sadness with the joy only youth can exude leaving an imprint behind as testament. When no youngsters were about it held the love of the ones who lived here with comfort, respect and contentment.

Battle between Good and Evil: Shirley's Story

Shirley and I first met while serving on jury duty in Warrenton. The jury was cloistered while the attorneys and judge worked out some details of the case pending. Somehow the subject of ghosts and hauntings came up. The room burst like a volcano becoming alive with discussion and comments on life after life. A short time later as we walked away from the building, Shirley said she had a story to tell me. Over lunch at the Southern City Grill I recorded her words

Shirley: It was many years ago when we were living in the country here in Warren County and when we still had outdoor toilets. So at night when I had to go out to the toilet, I noticed that every time I would walk through a warm spell and also when I was coming back, I'd go through the same warm spell.

After awhile one night I was lying in bed with my youngest daughter. She was about 13 or 14 months old at the time. She was sleeping and I was getting ready to go to sleep. I saw this masculine silhouette, the structure of a man. Around the head were little circles of lights flickering. It sat on the side of my bed. I did not want it there. I was afraid and yet I wasn't afraid. It sat there for a moment and said, "Kill your baby."

I said, "No."

And again it said, "Kill your baby."

I pulled her tight to me and strongly said, "No, she means too much to me." And it still sat there. I didn't know what to do then. It still kept sitting there. And a third time it said, "Kill your baby." I called out, "Please God, make this go away."

The way our house was, in the front was a south-facing window and on the side, a west facing window. He had come in from the west side. But at that moment when I pleaded with God to make this go away, from the south side an Angelic spirit came in. When it came through I heard an audible sound and then I heard an audible sound from the black silhouette. It stood up and I could hear audible sounds and as the Spiritual force came forth, that black silhouette of a man just ran out of the house.

The Spiritual force was not lit up but I could perceive it not as a man or woman but I felt it was a strong masculine being. I didn't see it outlined in any way but I could feel it there. It was a sense. I knew it was there.

At the time, it was in the news a lot, of people committing murders because of voices telling them to do that. I was shocked really when that happened to me. My husband was working out of town at the time and I stayed here with my four kids, so I was a little afraid. I didn't like being by myself again so my younger sister came to stay with me for awhile.

It let me know that beyond the shadow of a doubt, that there is more to life, more around us than we figure it to be. Even now sometimes there are evil spirits that try to come in to me but I don't allow them.

About seven years ago, maybe a little longer than that. It got to a point when I said to myself, "I'm gonna get out of here. I'm sick of this." Then it came to me, this is *my* house. God gave this to me. And I would pray. I bow down in front of my little altar when I would feel these bad spirits come right up to me. I would pray and it would go back. There was one that came to me that was a bossy type, like I felt he was saying, 'We're gonna get this lady.' He came in like he had more authority. He walked right up to me and he was pressing against me and I kept praying for it to go. It acted like it did not want to go back. I didn't move. I continued to pray then I felt it just move back away from me.

There was a time when every night a spirit would come out between my neighbor's house and mine. It was like a threat, as if to say, 'I'm coming.' That lasted about three or four months.

Later, some guests were in my house visiting because we were having a revival. For three nights this terrible loud noise outside my house like someone yelling in a foreign but satanic language. I couldn't understand the words. My guests heard that, too. It was horrific. It never came back. Sometimes people can bring those bad spirits into your house and your life. You just have to fight them off. I never invite people into my house if I think they carry bad spirits. I also have a personal relationship with God which all people need. It's important to ask God for help when you need it. The creaks in the house at night aren't always the house settling.

One night years later, I was expecting trouble from my abusive husband when he came home, so I told my son I wanted to sleep in his bed. He offered to sleep on the couch. A host of angels came to me. One would come up close to me and fade back then another would come up to me. I heard their wings fluttering. They were nurturing me. They did that and did that and did that. Then I thought I may as well go back to my own bed. I was comforted. I'll never forget that I had a host of angels around my bed protecting me.

During this period my husband had become more mentally abusive. One particular night I got up to go to the bathroom and check on the kids. I always checked on the kids but this night instead of seeing my husband, I *saw* a dark head with a whole lot of hair. I knew it wasn't my husband's persona that I saw when I got back into my bed. About ten years ago I went to Mariah Parham Hospital to visit somebody. I glanced into a room and saw that same dark head with all the hair. When he saw me he turned his head away. He was a patient lying in the bed. It was the same dark head. Some people carry dark spirits with them. Faith in the Lord will get you through."

Hardware Café Photo by Aaron Bukowski

A Mayor Returns: W.A. Miles Hardware Store

"Anyone who knew W.A. Miles Jr. knew how much he loved Warrenton, since he served as its Mayor for a total of 35 years and was still mayor when he passed away in 1997 one month away from his 80th birthday." This was a statement I heard from several people.

The W.A. Miles family roots in this area date back to patriot Dixon Marshall. He enlisted and served in the North Carolina Regiment of the Continental army to fight in the Revolutionary War. After he was taken prisoner in Charleston, South Carolina in 1780 he was exchanged and released the following year. Still he didn't quit fighting on his return but continued in the struggle for independence until the end of the War.

So began a long list of descendants delightfully happy being in Warren County and with W. A. Miles Jr. residing in Warrenton in particular. His grandfather, Alexander (called Alec) Major Miles was born in 1853. His wife, Sallie Snow Miles was that direct descendent (great granddaughter) of Dixon Marshall, Revolutionary War patriot. She was known to be a very religious Baptist. Statesman John H. Kerr wrote a memoriam for her when she died.

W. A. came to own the tin shop in Warrenton where he was quite well known and respected.

His son later expanded the Miles name in business on S. Main Street by opening the hardware store adjacent to his father's tin shop. Tin was popularly used for roofing at the time and later was formed and bent for use in downspouts, gutters, etc. Judge John Kerr's offices were on the second floor of the hardware store.

William Alexander Miles Sr. built his dream 2-story hardware store out of red brick in 1907. The building sat facing S. Main Street on a hill, so entrance to the rear basement was easily incorporated into use for merchandise delivered and picked up by the horses and wagons that were the standard use in that time. This actually made the building 3-stories high.

W. A. Sr. and Annie Lee Duke raised four children; W.A. Jr., Robert Duke, Randolph (called Dick) Marshall, and Sarah Elizabeth Miles. Sarah Miles (now) Johnson remembers, "Going to the Hardware store as a little girl and getting a nickel for candy from my daddy. He couldn't refuse me even in the early years of the depression because he was so happy to have a girl in the family after having three boys."

W. A. Miles Sr. passed away in 1941. His eldest son W. A. Jr. had completed one year of college (Carolina) but came home to run the hardware business. His brothers opted to fight in World War II leaving the business responsibility to their brother. Duke went into the Navy in January 1943 and Randolph (Dick) joined the Army in September of

1943 eventually becoming a Sergeant. When they returned after the war, they also worked in the hardware store.

W.A. Jr. married Gertrude Moore Draper. Their offspring were Sarah Ann Miles (Tate,) Tom and Beverly Miles (Drake.) Beverly began to tell me about her dad.

"We lived at the end of Fairview St. Dad walked to work most days, came home for lunch and walked back to work. He came home at six for dinner then usually went back to the store to do the bookkeeping or dressing the windows. I loved to do those big windows with him at least once a month. The windows were filled with hundreds of things for folks to look at.

"On the third floor they kept a lot of stock. I loved going up there with Daddy at night while he checked stock or worked on the books. I'd find all kinds of interesting things. I looked in the old trunk and in the nooks and crannies of the place. The basement was always kept just so, too. The neatest place in the world. Clean. He had a couch down there, too. The materials were hauled in by horse and wagon and later in trucks.

"While I was in high school my friends and I would stop in the store most days to get 25 cents for soda and candy. (This was a repeat performance of her Aunt Sarah's a generation earlier and for a nickel instead of a quarter.) I learned early which buttons to push on the heavy, giant cash register before cranking it to open it for the petty cash drawer, with my daddy's encouragement, of course.

"When my Uncles Duke and Dick Randolph returned from the war they also helped to run the store. In the '60s Duke left and went to work in the furniture business. Dick and Daddy stayed at the store but it was Daddy who did all the buying and really ran the store. Dick was a hard worker but Daddy loved the business. The store was in his blood. He loved it like no other."

Warrenton seemed to be the place for him, in the W.A. Miles Hardware Store. W.A. carried the personality of a man who loved people. It was obvious how much he loved the hardware store and Warrenton. The people in town responded by voting him in as Mayor for 35 years. He was involved in everything, including the enjoyment of going to all the cocktail parties in town.

Beverly continued, "When Dick died, Daddy hired a couple people to work but Daddy was the only one who knew where every little bit and piece was located. It was a wonderful store that had all those odds and ends. And if an item couldn't be found in the store, Daddy knew right where to look for it. He must have known his business because it supported a few families for many years.

"Daddy passed away in 1997 just a month away from being 80 in remarkably good health up until the last two weeks. That was exactly how he would have chosen it, if he had the choice, not wanting to be a burden. He continued to run the store right up until the end, telling my brother to lock the doors when he knew he couldn't go back to it. His great loves were the store and Warrenton. He grew up here and was actually Mayor when he died at nearly 80 years old."

Love of place goes beyond a person's life, so the family put covenants in the deed when they sold the historic W.A. Miles Hardware Store building to keep the front colors orange and black.

Will and Denise Perry bought the historic hardware store and turned it into the Hardware Café, opening on 6 October 2001. They serve delicious homemade desserts, fresh ground regular and flavored coffees and signature sandwiches reminiscent of hardware store items, i.e. the Hammer, the Ladder, the Washtub, Nuts 'n Bolts, Mousetrap, etc. served on in-house baked breads. The shelves have been left exactly the same as W.A. had them. The huge, antique cash register sits on the counter with Warrenton post cards, books and other tasteful items. The ladder remains resting against the high shelves. Bins that held nails and screws now hold Hardware Café tee shirts and more.

Antiques, collectibles and handmade placemats, napkins, aprons, quilts, etc. fill the shelves that held carpenter's tools, mechanic's tools, gardening supplies, and general hardware items for the home and business. The wood floor creaks as the customers fill up the restaurant for coffee & goodies, lunch and for dinner on Thursday and Friday nights. They cater ambrosial private parties on the premises and off.

So, the Hardware Café seems to be as successful as the W.A. Hardware Store. W.A. probably approves. In the early days of becoming a Café, a young lad working there scooted downstairs to bring supplies up to the kitchen when he *saw* W.A. sitting on the couch, relaxing. He sat on the same couch in the same clean, immaculate basement that he took pride in, four years after he *passed away*.

Kicking Up Ghosts   Photo by Aaron Bukowski

Wise

Restoration Kicks up the Ghosts: Todd's Story

One day every weekend Shawn and Todd enjoyed a day off from work that they used to explore North Carolina. One particular, picture-perfect fall day they headed north on I-85 to the last exit in the state, Hwy 1. Driving south from there, just poking along, they were enjoying the gorgeous scarlet, golden yellows and burnt ambers of the leaves falling from the trees, soaking in their favorite time of year.

    A couple miles down the road, the car slowed and stopped, seemingly by itself, in front of a house with a Preservation North Carolina sign in the yard. They pulled off the road and sat there, looking at this house for thirty minutes. They both felt a connection to the place.

"We were living very happily in a townhouse in North Raleigh. We weren't looking to re-locate and we weren't looking to buy anything. We were just enjoying a day out! I can't explain how this house drew us in and held us. The entire day was a kind of magical day." Todd tells anyone willing to listen.

Shawn said, "This is it. This is the house."

Todd replied quickly, "No, no. I don't think so."

That's how it all began. They called Preservation North Carolina but realized that they couldn't meet the guidelines demanded for the restoration of the house in the required time frame. Reluctantly, they put the idea aside.

Sometime later the sign was gone from the property. Shawn and Todd decided to stop in to talk to Eleanor, the owner.

"We made several visits with her, her daughter Debbie, her granddaughter, Destiny and her great granddaughter, Chrissie. It was a house of women. Debbie's husband Harvey was living in Durham."

All of them lived in the downstairs portion of the house, including their sleeping quarters. They were invited to explore upstairs.

"No one went with us. I didn't think anything of it at the time." Todd continued.

Each bedroom door was closed. We opened the first door at the front of the house. "The air was oppressive. The room was painted totally black, chalkboard black. Much later we learned that it was Debbie's son's room. He died in his late teens or early twenties. From there we roamed the other bedrooms, opening the closed doors to enter. I thought it was strange, to have the doors shut tight. Each bedroom was cold, dismal, like dead air. We left soon after."

We talked and talked about the house. Shawn felt strongly pulled toward the house. Eventually I was, too. We made several trips back.

On one of those trips they decided to ask Brian, a clairvoyant friend to accompany them.

"Brian was fascinated with the idea of the house. But as soon as we got inside the house and up the stairs again to the large expansive landing, he said, 'I feel a lot of tragedy, a lot of children, and a lot of things going on here. I can't stay here. I must go.' Our sensitive friend left immediately."

"Oh, m'gosh! What is going on?" We thought. We talked. Again we talked about the house and then again and again.

On our third visit before we talked about sale price, we asked, "Is there anything unusual going on in the house? Is there anything we should know?"

Debbie replied, "Why? Did you feel something?"

Todd thought that was an odd response to the question. She looked at her mother and her mother looked back at her and smiled. They said nothing. They obviously didn't want to scare us from buying the house.

Shawn and Todd talked about the house. The more they talked the more they felt like the house was calling to them. Perhaps this was meant to be. They both felt the house was beckoning to them, wanting them to be the owners, to live there and to care for it. Several trips to Wise occurred throughout the year before they made the offer to buy it.

The acre and a half property still has the two-story 1865 outdoor kitchens, the original barn and two outbuildings in the back.

Strangely enough Eleanor didn't want to make lots of money on the house. She wanted just enough to buy a doublewide for the lot next door where they planned to live.

Finally Shawn and Todd decided, yes, this house was meant for them. They went to the attorney's office and did all the traditional things accorded to buying a house. It was time to move in.

Todd said, "We rented U-hauls and began unloading and carrying stuff in. We nestled the washer and dryer in the foyer out of the way. I placed my large Craftsman toolbox on top of the dryer, squarely in the middle, knowing that I would need to use it and not wanting to search for it."

He continued, "We were standing near the foyer when Debbie came down the hallway to talk to us. The three of us stood there, Debbie was about to speak, when out of the corner of my eye, I saw the toolbox lift up, the (latched) lid opened up and turned to dump its entire contents onto the floor!"

"Did you see that?" Debbie was as dumbfounded as we were!

Not one of them could explain what just happened! That was the true beginning of their experiences of weird happenings in the house. Todd always knew there were unexplainable events that happen in life and in the world. He never experienced any until that very moment.

As time passed, they lived with other oddities. Voices in the night, waking them from a deep sleep, yet when they woke to listen; the voices stopped. Several times the door in the dining room that opens to the foyer slammed so loudly that they thought someone had broken into the house! They would lie in bed, scared stiff that a stranger invaded their home. Yet in the morning when they crept downstairs, the door would be standing open, just as they left it the night before. Not a thing was out of place.

These events grimly bothered Todd. He noticed a difference in the dogs' behavior. They were seriously affected. Todd got really upset. The dogs became greatly reactionary. When they were all in the TV room, Paws' hair would suddenly stand on end and he'd rise up, stare into space and begin barking---at nothing they could see! Or he'd fly off the ottoman chasing something into the hallway where he'd pause looking from side to side with nothing visible insight.

Day after day when Todd and Shawn came home after work, the dogs' eyes were encrusted. Todd knew they'd been crying all day. He'd gently clean away their eyes in agony knowing they were suffering but not knowing what to do about it. The dogs were really unsettled by all the unclear calamities happening.

A friend suggested Shawn and Todd talk to the entities. They did.

In the meantime, Debbie's husband Harvey had moved back into their home next door. He'd stop over and ask, "Is everything okay? Any problems? Are you guys doing alright?"

It was then that they heard the story of when Chrissie was a little girl she was standing at the bottom of the stairs, aiming a toy gun at the top of the steps.

"Chrissie, what are you doing?" she was asked.

"I'm going to shoot the man in the blue suit up there." There was no man visible to anyone else.

After hearing of this incident Shawn and Todd recalled the black room. It was the only bedroom where none of the clothing was removed before the house became theirs. In the closet hung a gray suit--------and a blue suit!

"I think many odd things went on in the house that we weren't told about. Debbie did say that she slept in the bedroom across from the 'black' bedroom. She had to prop the door open at night or the door would forcibly close tight shutting out any air flow."

"We still have the original copper and brass door escutcheons. You have to pull really hard to shut the doors. They don't just close on their own. Personally, I think that's when they stopped sleeping upstairs. The whole family moved downstairs to sleep."

After being in the house for six months or so, Shawn's mother came to visit from Florida. They carried her luggage into the Gray room, which is behind the front, Black room. The next morning she was a bit quiet, complacent. Todd and Shawn thought she was tired from traveling because she was looking so pensive.

"Something very strange happened to me last night. I almost feel like I want to get my plane ticket home."

"Mom, what's wrong? What's going on?"

"It felt like some 'thing' was on top of me. I couldn't breathe. I just couldn't catch my breath. When I rolled onto my side, I felt breathing on my face. I'm scared! I tried to scream for you to help me and nothing audible would come out of my mouth. I couldn't speak!"

Shawn and Todd went upstairs to the Gray room. The bed was freshly made up yet a deep depression was on one side of the bed including the pillow, as if someone were still lying there!

As time went by they learned that the Gray room had more 'paranormal' activity than any other room in the house.

Other members of Shawn's family came for visits. His sister reported hearing the rattle of dice before it was tossed and rolled across a surface. Feminine voices always accompanied that sound. Later they found that Blanche Hayes, Malvern's (a former owner) second wife was an avid, big-time Bridge player. There were lots of card games and soiree's going on in the house when they lived here. She was well known in Warren County for her socials. Needless to say, none of Shawn's family would sleep upstairs except Aunt Caroline.

Shawn's Aunt Caroline was intrigued by whoever was with her in the Gray room. The entity played with her hair dryer. On. Off. On. Off. She ran downstairs to report an electrical problem with her light switch. It, too, went on, off, on, off. Shawn and Todd followed her upstairs and watched the light switch---all by itself---go on, off, on, off. Without a body in sight.

Aunt Caroline became fascinated with the entity playing with her. And she kept playing back. She'd stay upstairs for hours, verbalizing with --------whoever it was! She was completely intrigued.

Antagonisms continued. Some episodes occurred to Shawn and Todd. Different experiences happened to friends and family.

"As we continued to make changes in the house, replacing rotted floorboards and such, we noticed the 'paranormal' activity lessened. Voices ceased for a while before starting up again."

One day Todd was in the house alone, with the dogs, when he heard very clearly- enunciated 'Todd' spoken into his ear. Just his name, 'Todd'. He told himself, "I didn't hear that." Then it happened again. When he told Shawn, he replied, "I didn't want to scare you, so I didn't tell you, but it's happened to me, several times." They never could figure that out. Who, what or why? As soon as they acknowledged to each other that it happened, it never happened again.

"I woke up one day in the Blue Room when I had the same experience as Shawn's mom. The Blue Room is where Eleanor's mother passed away. My breathing stopped and it jolted me awake. I couldn't catch my breath. I was struggling to breathe.

"I went next door to Debbie. She revealed that she'd been dozing on the couch in that room - it was set in the same spot as our sofa – when she woke to see a vision of a young boy standing next to her. It was the only experience of that kind that ever happened to her in the house.

"It kind of scared me. I really want to see something but it's never revealed itself to me in that form.

"Our house was built in 1901. In 1920 the kitchen we have now was attached to the main building. In the days of long ago, the 'slave house' or kitchen was where they prepared food because of their fear of fire to the big house. The food was carried into the house to serve it. When the connection between the two was made, they built a breezeway between the actual home and the kitchen. Clapboards and the boarded up windows remained. The old water heater and our – then – washer sat there.

"In this breezeway one of the exterior doors had plastic stapled over it. Plastic was above, too. I didn't like it but knew we would address that in time to come, revealing that exterior. I stood in the breezeway with all the lights turned off in the house. I was completely alone, when I saw this milky, watery kind of image. It was thickly milky so that I almost couldn't see through it. And it was right in front of me! The minute I recognized that this shouldn't be there in front of me and it registered with me just what I was seeing, it vaporized upwards. The plastic on the door pulled forward and let go as it would if air were passing through the house. That's the only time I saw an image of something that I couldn't understand.

"I've had a series of things unusual and different that has happened. I remember when we bought the house in April of 2001. I opened my business on South Main Street in Warrenton that year. It got around that these people had bought a house in Wise and planned to change the exterior of the white house with black shutters. I wanted Butter Yellow with Forest Green shutters.

"This caused a stir in the community. Whispers came to me, 'I hope you're not going to change that house, it's always been that way.'

His reply, "We're paying the mortgage, we're choosing the colors, period." The crew of painters began right away. Folks did take notice.

A young woman walked into his store with her story. "As a little girl I used to play in that house but it terrified me. Everybody that tried to go upstairs would always trip or fall by the time they got to the second landing, maybe even pushed down the stairs. I sprained my ankle so badly that I didn't want to go back into the house again. There was always activity in that stairwell."

She paused and then continued. "When we did sleepovers, we brought tents to sleep in, outside, never in the house."

Todd continued, "I was starting to hear some terrible things that made me a bit unsure. Did we do the right thing in buying this house?

There was some hint that maybe some terrible things happened in the Gray Room involving an older man. There seems to be a heavy female connection. The women coming into my store to tell me of their encounters as young girls that made them so uncomfortable that they didn't want to return to it, in the house we recently purchased, made me pause for thought.

"Eleanor's father convalesced in the Gray Room. That may have set the tone for the girls being afraid. But there was always activity in that room. The family later told us of the chair that rocked – by itself with no one in it– in that room. That's the reason Destiny stopped sleeping there and slept downstairs instead. It seems each person had happenings in their bedrooms that made them eventually leave them to sleep downstairs.

"It was a bit weird, to have strangers come into my store to tell me stories of odd encounters in our house. We were new to the store, to the house and to the area. That can be a bit unnerving.

"Harvey revealed that he didn't want to be alone in the house, anymore. He's a plumber by trade and was working on the plumbing upstairs. Debbie was out shopping. He felt like something really heavy was on his back. He couldn't wait to get downstairs, he ran until he was outside the house. The heavy thing stayed on his back until he got outside then it was gone. He never stayed inside the house alone again.

"Harvey and Debbie still live next door. Sometimes when he won't come over, he'll wave to us from their yard. Those times he says he can feel a presence where we are in the yard. He also sees images on the front porch at night.

"The strange part about that is that we began to think maybe he was embellishing his stories a bit---for dramatic purpose. Then Shawn's sister, Cammie and her husband Steve came for a visit for the first time. Steve has never experienced any paranormal moments at all, until his father passed away. Steve was in the hospital room at the time and felt his father's spirit pass through him. Since then he became in tune with certain happenings even having interpretive dreams that he witnessed come true.

"They were all on the porch early in the evening, sitting at one end of it. The porch is 700 square feet with 12 columns. It's a big front porch.

"Steve was staring at the other end of the porch when he murmured, 'I see an aura. I'm seeing outlines and images standing at the far end.' They didn't stay with us that night but later when they returned, he continued. 'I don't sense any evil or bad. I see colors of blue and yellow. I just can't deal with it right now. I'm still adapting to this new ability that has come to me.'"

Shawn and Todd talked Steve into coming back to stay with them again. He had no issues when he did return. They found it interesting that he had seen the same images Harvey told them about. Everyone seems to have stories about the past and even the present to tell Todd and Shawn.

"I feel that instead of us finding this house, the house found us. I also believe that it's important to listen to a house. If something is wrong, the house will find a way to tell us. I'm sure the house is directing us. We painted the entire downstairs and the foyer going up. I chose a camel-back soft yellow, a very historic, National Trust color. I was sure it would give the house such lightness. A couple weeks later the color was bothering me. I talked to Shawn.

"It's been bothering me, too. It's just not the right color." Shawn said.

Todd continued telling me. "I can't believe we made such a mistake on this color. The ceilings are 12-foot high and we ran up the staircase with it, wrapping it around. That's a lot of painting."

Next they chose a beautiful soft grayish-sage green. Instantly there was calm.

The downstairs bathroom was the last room in the house that needed restoring. Before the contractor came Todd pulled a built-in cabinet off the wall. The urge to do that dropped on him like a thirsty man needing water. The wall behind the cabinet revealed the original color-sage green. Then Todd realized that sage green was the color behind other items they've pulled away from the walls.

The right color was there all the time. It needed to be uncovered. The house spoke to them, leading them to the right color.

Todd said, "As we do demolition and renewal of the house, I take photographs to record everything. Shawn took the buzz saw to cut up the kitchen floor. It was all rotted with water dampness. I took the photographs of the saw blade throwing saw dust up and away. The photos were filled with perfectly round, little, yellow circles; orbs. I took several series of photos that day. That was the only one where orbs showed up.

"I mentioned this to Harvey. He told me that when Garth was still alive, he and Harvey went under the house to do some plumbing work in that same location. That's when frightening events began to happen in the house.

The granite foundation of the house came from the same Paschall brothers-owned quarry here in Wise that sent granite to Washington D.C. for use in building the Pentagon and other great buildings there. One of the Paschall brothers was the builder of our house.

The house was not originally built for Malvern Hayes; it was built for one of three millionaires, the first in the county, of the mercantile business.

Todd tells me, "I don't like cemeteries. I just don't. I don't like to talk about death either. But I did feel that we should go to Wise Cemetery to find Malvern's gravesite. Sort of adding a dot over an i. We were not there five minutes as if we were drawn to the very spot of Malvern's resting place." Todd's now aware that he has small moments of psychic abilities. They have both come to understand they are sharing their home with former residents and believe the spirits appreciate the work they have done to the house.

Author's Note: More than a year after this interview, maybe even closer to two years, I unexpectedly ran into Todd. With a twinkle in his eye, he confided that he had a post script to his story to tell me. "Just recently," he said, "I was settled in a chair sound asleep in the den. I had dozed off and was in one of those deep slumbers. The dogs were out of it, too. Suddenly, my eyes popped wide open as I tried to take a deep breath almost choking. An image was close before me, rather free-formed, curvy, black at the top and purple below it. I sensed it was female but have no reason to say that. It took only a second and it was gone. Poof!"

Johnny Reb, Indians and More: Nancy's Story

How people arrived in places they live in, has always intrigued me. So my interview with Nancy began with her reasons for moving to Wise, North Carolina. She filled me in on the bad year for hurricanes in Florida that left her and her husband dismayed with living in a lovely home boarded up for five months of the year. That being their defense against a seemingly angry Mother Nature encouraged them to look further for a home to enjoy.

They explored the real estate sections online offering homes for sale in northeastern Georgia; eastern, but not coastal South Carolina and Piedmont North Carolina. Wise, North Carolina, on a quiet street with only five houses is where they chose to settle. Using the proceeds made from the sale of their Florida home paid for the improvements on their new, 71 year-old house.

Nancy begins, "The first year we were here while I was in my second floor computer room, I looked down out of the window to the big shed and saw a figure, a man, in drab clothing, gray, with his head turned slightly so I could see his cap (Civil War Confederate enlisted man's Forage cap) with the round top tipped forward. At first I thought it was my neighbor walking across my property. I was focused on his upper body then realized that I couldn't see anything below his knees. He then faded and I knew I hadn't seen a live person.

"I'm not afraid of things like that. I stayed with my husband in upstate New York, in his mobile home before we moved to Florida. We were lying in bed when I saw an Indian with black hair in a braid or two, I couldn't tell how many, and a feather hanging down in back. (Nancy indicated another feather or two sticking out the side also.) He had a blanket or drapery-kind of thing on his shoulders. He walked past the window. The windows were high up off the ground and it was nearly night time. At first I was startled because I thought it was someone sneaking around our house.

"I asked if there were any people around dressed like Indians. He had me describe him and then said that these people were seen all the time and were not a positive thing. We moved shortly after that experience, not for that reason but because we had plans to move to a warmer climate."

On second thought Nancy realized that their windows *were* too high up from the ground for anyone to just be walking by and being seen by her.

Onondaga and Oneida tribes were located in the Oswego area of New York and would have been dressed as Nancy described. Both tribes were of the Iroquois confederacy, traditionally non-aggressive people. Both also had a long history in the area that had always been famous for its salmon fishing.

In their new home, they also talked to neighbors about paranormal phenomena.

"One neighbor has told my husband that he can periodically smell his late mother's perfume," Nancy continued noting that she too, smells a perfume in the air but doesn't know what scent his mother wore. "He lives alone with many dogs and cats, roaming around at night so he is in tune and aware of things others are not. One time, outside, he saw a large dark apparition floating around in the trees. It unnerved him.

"Another neighbor said many years ago when she was small, she saw from her upstairs window a group of people walking from the direction of where the railroad used to be. The area was open and clear of growth then. They strolled toward her house, entered the front door, without opening it, walked right through it and out the other side, disappearing."

Nancy continued with her own happenings. "My experiences have been mostly auditory and sensory. I can smell food, ham baking, yeast rolls, sweet tobacco, and very sweet tobacco, like the kind they used to grow before they began putting all the additives in it. Last fall some people stopped in who had lived in our house. Only four families ever lived here. Perkinson was their name. The boy said his mother was *always* baking pies and cooking ham. I hear sounds in the house, not settling sounds or footsteps but like a door scraping when opening, but not latching, dropping sounds like something falling off a shelf. But when I go upstairs, nothing is out of place.

"And I hear music, a lot. So does my husband. I hear barber shop quartets and the Andrews Sisters-type melody. I don't hear the words but the music. My husband hears band music.

"He is developed psychically. When he lived in New York he listened to his neighbor whose husband had died. She would conduct Voodoo to recall her husband. Then she had conversations with him. She also got angry if she thought my husband was listening to both of them. He said there was a portal of blackness around this place where he lived and time would be missing periodically. At one point big dogs chained to their doghouses actually pulled their doghouses away, out of that area. Even the farm animals ran away.

"One time at our house (that we lived in later) we had old wooden shutters that closed over the windows. He was taking the Shutter Dogs off; they are the "S" shaped hardware that keeps the shutters from flapping in the wind. Old original hardware is valuable. He was stripping it off when suddenly it was wrenched out of his hands, spun on its end like in a whirlwind, around and around, dropped to the ground and broke into every piece possible.

"Something even more frightening, a few weeks ago we took our 30-foot RV, the kind you sit in front to drive like a bus, we took it in to be serviced and the first thing they worked on was the generator. The first stop we made, we put the generator on and it wouldn't work. My husband was fit to be tied because we had taken it to the same place we'd been to before and had trouble with it.

"After that, it worked fine. One morning my husband let the dogs out at 7 o'clock. He heard the RV running in the driveway and thought how really strange that was. He got the keys because the RV was locked up and there was no way to turn the generator from the outside. He turned it off. Later the neighbor told him that he had heard the motor running at 4 o'clock one morning. That was weird.

"The next day my husband went outside and while standing there, he watched the whole RV shudder, all by itself just like a dog would shake water from its back. Then it stopped. It had not been running."

Nancy knows her husband is psychically developed. Before they moved in, he came up from Florida early to clean and to purify the house by smudging. This is a ritual that many people do before moving into a house.

Tightly bound sage forms a smudge stick. You light one end with a candle while holding the other in your hand, blowing out any flame. It is the smoke that absorbs the negative energy dissolving it when the smoke dissolves. This cleanses each room of negative spirits as you walk around the perimeter clockwise paying special attention to closets, corners and behind doors. This can also be done periodically to chase negative emotions from your home, too. You can also use Mugwort (a sage) to enhance psychic energy and lavender to bring balance, peacefulness and loving energy into the home. Mugwort has long been used by Native Americans and Celtic peoples.

After the purification, Nancy's husband spoke to the spirit of the house, asking if there were anything bad about the house or anything they should be concerned about. He felt a positive reaction that there was nothing to be afraid of. Nancy feels the same way, stating "I'm not afraid to be in my house. I have lived in a place that I was afraid in. It was a very old house that had a cellar that 'breathed.' But in this house, I have no fears at all."

The Putnam House   Photo by Aaron Bukowski

Warren Plains

Children's Tea Party: The Putnam Story

The *ghost children* in the Putnam household told Alice to invite me to tea. "Delighted," I replied. This would be a brand new experience for me. I have been invited to Tea and I have seen a ghost child but this combination was a first. I looked forward to going with much anticipation.

A bright, sunny dawn began this Monday the 14th of February. It was Valentine's Day, at 2 p.m. that I arrived with a box of French Mint Chocolates in hand.

Tri, a two year old German shepherd mix dog, greeted me at the door, sniffing me properly until he was certain that I was a friend not a foe. Wagging his tail, he followed along while Alice led the way to the *children's* room. A lovely silver tea set was in place with a small plate of cookies on a child's table. I opened my box of chocolates and set them down. A few stuffed African-American folk dolls, Victorian porcelain dolls dressed in exquisite finery, baby dolls, flip dolls and a variety of teddy bears filled the little alcove from wall to wall. Some sat on chairs, some on the window ledge and some sat on benches, etc.

Alice and Tri left me to enjoy the party. I sat in total silence, relaxing, waiting. Not a sound could I hear in this hundred year old house. Not a creak, not a floor board, not a whisper from the blowing winds whipping across the fields surrounding the house was heard. Not even a mouse.

Photo from the author's collection. All ready and waiting for the Children's Tea Party to begin.

A tingling started on my hands and moved up my arms, my eyesight adjusted briefly to almost a blur. I talked gently to the *children* I knew were in this tiny room with me, thanking them for inviting me. I continued, waiting patiently for a response. I ate a cookie for politeness. Then I felt the weight of a child sitting on my shoulders as children love to do. There was no coldness or change of temperature; no noise. Just peace. Then a mild pressure to my chest as though I were holding a child against it. I reacted without words, just letting it happen. The moments passed. I have no idea how long I sat in this charming little tea room with the *spirits* of happy children. I sat for possibly an hour before I heard sounds floating up from the downstairs.

Tri's claws danced on the steps and floor as he came up to check on me. The Tea Party ended on that note. We removed to the downstairs front withdrawing room.

Duane brought in mugs of good hot coffee while we sat on the antique couch in this comfortable women's room. An old stone fireplace adorned the far wall. Gorgeous chandeliers hung from the ceilings and tiffany style lamps added brilliant color throughout.

My first question was, "Where did you live before coming to Warrenton?" Alice surprised me by saying, "Warrenton, Virginia from a house that was also a hotbed of paranormal activity." Intrigued, I asked for more details. She began to tell me.

"Our last home was built by the Hutton family in 1887 on Falmouth Street and is now considered in the Historic District."

My research shows me that Henry Isaac Hutton was born on 24 March 1859 in Fairfax County, Virginia. He became an insurance agent before marrying Mae Grace Halley of Anacostia, Maryland on 19 June 1889. She had a daughter, Josephine Alifero Broders born in 1887, with Joseph Perrin Broders. He passed away in 1888.

Hutton built his home on Falmouth Street when it was still called East Main, probably in anticipation of marrying. Henry and Mae Grace produced three children, Margaret 1890–1982; Elizabeth Kulp 1891–1990; and Edmund Henry 1897–1935. Her parents, the Halleys, also lived with them.

When Josephine became a young lady, she made some social visits to her aunt, Mrs. Charles Creighton Carlin of North Washington Street in Washington D.C. for social events. Mr. Carlin was a member of the House of Representatives. In 1912 Josephine took her still unmarried step-sister Elizabeth with her to the Musicale and Dance at the Elks Home where 400 people attended. Mrs. Leroy Baxley and Miss Jane Bell were also guests in the Carlin household that week.

Josephine married Llewellyn Wood, traveled to Boston, Massachusetts; New York City, New York; Naples, Italy; and to San Juan, Puerto Rico where her purpose was to nurse someone ill. She returned to Warrenton, Virginia to live and remained there after becoming a widow. She passed away in 1973 possibly living with the Hutton family.

Margaret had married Dr. Robert Edward Ferneyhough on 19 Oct 1910 when she was twenty years old; he was twenty-seven. He was a veterinarian and already owned his house on Lee Avenue. They issued a daughter Mae Livinia and son Robert Jr. who passed away at fifteen years of age. Ferneyhough had a child from his previous marriage but the child did not live with them. Dr. Robert lived until 1971 and Margaret until 1982 just five years before her daughter passed away.

Henry Isaac and Mae Grace's son Edmund Henry had passed away at thirty-eight years of age in 1935.

But daughter Elizabeth never married. She remained in the house with her parents. Her mother passed away in 1944 and her father in 1954. The house was left to her. She sold it in the 60's to Becky Adams, retaining rights to a part of the house for as long as she wanted.

Alice picked up the conversation again saying, "Duane and I were married about a month when we traveled up from New Orleans because of a transfer at Duane's work and were looking for a house. An old house. The first real estate agent in Virginia was showing us houses built in the 1960s in the Manassas area. That's not quite what we had in mind. I knew that a home in Maryland was not the right place for us.

"A friend suggested we look in a particular area in Virginia. As I scanned the map with my finger between Fredericksburg and the Culpepper area my hand started to shake visibly. Someone was guiding me to Warrenton, I'm sure. So we had an agent show us the Hutton house in Warrenton. As we went up the back stairs, I said to Duane, 'I think Lizzi (she pronounces it Liz-eye) is still in the house, do you mind?' I hadn't really told him about this part of myself that feels things. He said, 'Fine.' And that was that.

"The house had been on the market for eight months. The evening after we signed contracts on it, (to buy it) the agent received a call from a doctor in Pennsylvania who had been waiting to sell his house to buy this one. His just sold. But I think the house had been waiting for us."

Joe Winkelmann of the Fauquier Times-Democrat newspaper wrote an article on the Putnam's experience in the house. The newspaper printed a photo with it that shows the image of a woman's face, presumably Elizabeth, in the mirror above the fireplace mantel.

At the time, Alice prepared to paint the front room, second floor which was Lizzi's sitting room. She placed her cup of coffee on the mantel as she began working. Within seconds the cup clattered to the floor spewing coffee all over like a tidal wave. Alice watched it go. It didn't slip off, it had momentum. After that, whenever Alice went into the room for any reason she called out that she was the maid coming to clean the room. Surely Elizabeth's ghost would accept that reason for intruding into her domain.

"The house included two apartments besides our living area. Dennis, who runs the Carousel Ice Cream, rented the back apartment. I asked him if his grandmother had moved in with him because he noticed pictures and things had been moved to different places. At first he said, 'Oh. Ya. My grandmother is always in my heart.' I said no, no. I mean did she *move in with you*. Very quietly he said, 'Oh, ya. I guess she did.'

"I figured she would be company for Lizzi. The house was hot with paranormal activity."

I returned to the Putnam household ten days after the Tea Party to pick up some information Alice found on the Wilker family. She invited me to take a moment to go upstairs to say hello to the *children* before I went on my way. I did. As before Tri escorted me up the stairs like the perfect guide dog. I sat in the same chair I sat in before, breathed deeply to relax and said quietly, "Hello again. I'm just taking a moment to say 'Hello' to you." At that very moment, a blur crossed my eyes and I felt pressure against my chest. The same as ten days earlier. It rather reinforced my first impression because I am always second guessing myself as in, "Did I really? Could I have imagined?"

Duane and Alice bought this house in Warren Plains in 2005. The first impressions Alice received when she entered the house were of parties, social gatherings of their large families. As Alice and Duane started coming to the house regularly (they did not move in right away) she heard sounds of movement upstairs when she was downstairs and *saw* colored lights floating across the walls with no explanation of where they were coming from.

Her psychic friend Janet said that she felt the family made some kind of liqueurs possibly from their orchards that she *saw*. She also said Alice may be a reincarnation of a girl who lived here (in the area, this house was not built then) during the War Between the States. She hears footsteps of the past, imprints of past lives that were here. Alice finds herself waltzing around the house. That's something she has never done before.

Photo by Duane Putnam. A ghostly being caught on camera in front of the Putnam home?

They traveled from Virginia usually every other Friday to do some work in the house, always with respecting the sensitivity of the house. Believing the house is a living entity and responding to anything that affects it, they were concerned about the physical work that had to be completed. The building itself reacted with alarm when the heating men began ripping out the old humongous oil furnace and out-of-date-ductwork. The house just shuddered and shook. The energy change could be felt. Alice said, "I could feel the house's spirit become angry with all the activity. We talked to the house, telling it that soon the destruction would be over and peace would reign again.

"In December we put a Christmas tree up adorned with lights." Alice continues. "We turned the lights off before going to bed. In the morning the tree lights would be on. When we went out to an auction, we turned the lights off thinking of safety before beauty. When we returned the tree lights were shining brightly. Comments were made to us about how pretty the lighted tree looked in the window as people drove by. It was always a time when we were not in North Carolina so we knew the lights were supposed to be shut off."

The curious, playful spirits used to set off the burglar alarm until Alice explained to them the consequences their actions could cause.

Alice picks up the thread of her thoughts. "The energy feels as though the family that lived here was very happy. When I first walked into the house I felt the parties, family gatherings.

"Sometimes we work with our friend Janet, an animal communicator for our dogs. She's very psychically talented and explained that some spirits came through the house, not staying but almost like being hermetically sealed in a unit so they don't leave any imprint on the house. She also said two women who are guarding the house screens strangers the first time they enter. A third, much younger lady also watches. At times I can feel the energy shifts in the house."

Alice continued, "At a yard sale I bought some jungle camouflage fatigue uniforms, to donate to the Loaves and Fishes. I spread them out on the sofa. The next day I sensed that one of the presences in the house is an old soldier. He was an Army gunnery sergeant or someone in control of troops. But he is an old soul. I *picked up* a group of military on the property who had recently died. This old soldier was helping them."

Duane added, "It was like a way station where spirits would stop for a rest on their way from one place to another. There was a vortex under the house in Virginia."

"The Marines passed through here on the way to the other side. They didn't seem to be healed enough because they were too soon *passed*. The Master/Gunnery was helping them to *pass over*. It took me awhile to figure out what was going on. But they wanted to go back, to find someone in their unit that they could *work* with, to communicate with, if there was an issue or problem that needed addressing. This was their mission before passing to the other side.

"The military were very obliging. When I asked them to leave the house, they did. Another time a large group of Army soldiers were here."

Almost as a postscript, Alice added, "I have this rule in my house. I don't want to see or hear them. I don't want to wake up in the middle of the night and trip over somebody." Apparently the ghosts ignore her rule or sometimes make a mistake. She has seen a man in a chocolate wool waistcoat. A part of a man anyway. It was just from the waist up.

The first kin to live at this address were the Andreas Wilker family. He was born in 1828 in Grebanau, Germany of parents Johannes Peter and Margaret Kaulbfleish Wilker. He immigrated to the rural area of Woodstock, Ontario, a town of 1000 people in Canada, where he married Elizabeth Bynum (Baumann). She was a native Canadian born on Christmas Day in 1834 of German descent parents. The area became known as the Dairy Capital of Canada and a Friendly City. It had been settled around 1800 by many Americans arriving from New York. The town also produced an American Civil War Medal of Honor winner, Benjamin Franklin Youngs.

Wilker followed the Lutheran doctrine as most Germans did at the time. His wife later joined the Warren Plains Baptist Church. Andreas eventually became a Presbyterian. However they are buried in the Old Warrenton Cemetery. Their son Andrew is buried at Warren Plains.

They traveled back to Germany possibly as a honeymoon trip. Their first born, Katrina was born there in 1853. They returned to Woodstock for the birth of their second child, Leonard in 1855. Margaret, Henry, Adam, Andrew, Christina, Elizabeth (Lizzie) were also born in Woodstock. In 1874 daughter Nancy Carolina was born in Warren County, North Carolina.

Wilker was a farmer in Canada when he purchased 244 acres to continue farming in Warren Plains. A cotton gin and sawmill were supposedly later added to his holdings. The family had left Zorra West, Oxford North, in Woodstock, Ontario, Canada. All the children remained in North Carolina except Nancy who married Will Thompson and moved to Spartanburg, South Carolina. The house and farm were sold to the Connell family ca. 1912.

William A. and Mae Beardsley Connell bought the property, brought their family to the house in Warren Plains after a fire burned their home at the Fork in Inez. They owned a large farm where he planted mostly cotton and continued to farm the land in Inez after the move. He, too, was a Canadian by birth coming from the same area as the Wilker family; Elizabeth emigrated from Ireland, also the land of his forefathers.

***

Alice and Duane decided to have professionals come out to uncover their household spirits. G.H.O.S.T.S. of Raleigh, Beth and Don invited two other paranormal research teams, The Heritage Hunters Society and N.C.H.A.G.S. to join them in the investigation. These paranormal observers like to share their information and experiences. Tess walked through and stated that one ghost tends to move things around. There is nothing bad or vicious about her spirit. An 18 year old male also made an impression. Tess also smelled smoke like the smoke from a house fire at one time. Andreas Wilker, the patriarch of the family appeared to her.

Steve felt a shock when they first entered the historic house. Something or someone zapped him in the middle of his back.

The group held a Paranormal PX in the woman's parlor where they asked questions and recorded energy sounds they interpreted. All electricity was turned off in the house at the time. Eddie and Mike watched in riveted fascination as a cordless phone leapt off its base and landed on Eddie's chest.

Mike experienced a sharp pain as if a knife was jabbed into his right shoulder blade. While still in the parlor another really physically fit, strong member of their group got a sharp pain in his chest. At first they thought it was a heart attack, but it went away immediately. Alice told them that an owner died of a heart attack in that room. None of the teams considered themselves psychically developed. They depend purely on their equipment to sense the spirits of the place.

Alice put on a spread for the ghost hunters. The table was laden with salads, sandwiches and other enticing foods. Al was sitting at a small table adjacent. He leaned over to speak, while he was turned away, his bowl of salad flew off the table to where it sat as neat as a picture. Unfortunately the cameras and sensors were turned off.

Interview with a Ghost Hunter:
Michael La Chiana of THHS

After receiving the Putnam's permission, I contacted Michael La Chiana of The Heritage Hunters Society asking if we could meet to discuss their haunted household. We each brought different experiences to the table. Michael has the technical knowledge using specialized equipment and experience from his many visits to haunted sites that he has on record. I offered my personal experiences and those from the paranormal stories I've been collecting for many years. Non-stop talk went on for over two hours. We still had not depleted what we had to share.

Michael, along with his investigators from THE HERITAGE HUNTERS SOCIETY were invited to visit the Putnam home by good friends Beth and Don Wilson of G.H.O.S.T.S. of Raleigh to offer the best paranormal research to a property owner. NC HAGS works with the group as well. The three teams respect each other's work, doing their research as a service to the community and to further understand the *unseen* that affect ours. Neither of these groups charges a fee.

Each group has their own guidelines and use different equipment, reporting the information they receive in a manner of their own. Together they form a picture from various angles of their visit to haunted places, seeking unknown truth for those of us interested in paranormal activity and the history behind it. If an incident can be explained as normal circumstances, they offer their understanding of it.

THHS uses a relaxed atmosphere where a feeling of camaraderie prevails. This is a bit different from some other ghost hunting groups who charge into a building with bravado. Fame and notoriety is not what they seek. This also may be the reason they are so successful in having the spirits respond and sometimes talk to them. It is recorded in explicitly clear voices but not always. Michael tends to return to the place by himself utilizing silence and patience to attract the more shy spirits that hang about a place. He also makes small video movies to share with the public when there is good evidence of a haunting.

One of the first things I learned from Michael is that old wiring emits leakage that can affect energy in a house and the health of the people living there. He explained to me about Spike from VMF and K-11 meters that pick up electrical current emissions. So he takes meter readings of the whole house after asking where the 'hot spots' of the house are located. These would be the areas of the most activity. Then he shuts the power off completely. With no electrical power in the house, their equipment still kept picking up high readings in the

Putnam house. Photo by Duane Putnam. An unidentified entity in the Putnam home.

"I'm very methodical," Michael continued telling me his methods and explaining the tools he uses. "The digital cameras and audio recorders pick up sights and sounds that we cannot hear and see. I even use something as simple as wind chimes by hanging them in the center of a room with no drafts. Perfect stillness is necessary. Movement of energy will set the chimes a tinkling. I have put many original ideas to use over the years. It's challenging."

It is also his habit to walk the whole property inside and out. He employs several recording devices at the same time. Sometimes one will pick up what another will not.

"I was called in on a case of a two-year old house that people were renting. The small sub-division was built on old farmland way out in the country. They were ready to move out, trying to break their lease so they could get away from this home. The wife was hysterical. The husband was kind of babbling, running around in circles with a bible in his hands. Then they were frantically throwing everything that was theirs into a U-Haul and left. They begged us to keep the spirits there as they left. That was their only concern. They did not want to be contacted, even if we found any proof.

First we set up all our gear and did EMF readings before killing the power. Everyone then spread out and was told to be quiet. We call this 'Ghost Watching.' Nothing much was recorded at first. We stayed several hours. I went upstairs to a big walk-in closet in the bathroom and sat there running audio and taking photos in the dark. Then my camera malfunctioned. Battery drainage is common when spirits are around. Upon review of my recorder the following day, I realized I captured a woman saying, 'Is he taking a picture of me?' That was a really good EVP. It blew my mind. Some of the others heard some whispers in this location earlier in the evening.

I even recorded first and last names that have actually come through. That is very rare. We had been downstairs getting high readings on our meters that indicated something going on. I just wandered away from everybody and went into a corner and quietly said, 'Tell me your name. Next I clearly heard from out of a different realm, 'Lee Bloom,' on my recorder. A few minutes later, I asked again and recorded, 'Katie Morgan.'

When someone gives you a first and last name, you can try to backtrack and research old records. Two different women gave me their full names. I don't know of anyone who has ever recorded a capture like these. That was an amazing night for me as a paranormal investigator."

History and paranormal go hand in hand and Michael is also interested in history. He is owner of Heritage Plumbing Company, a full service, licensed plumbing business serving the Raleigh/Durham areas since 1992, who does modern plumbing amenities but also specializes in old and historical home plumbing restorations and appearances. He can turn a modern bathroom into a Victorian appearance with modern facilities.

"We've done many hotels, inns, B & Bs, restaurants, resorts and even an antique store. There are certain cases THHS will not do. I'm not into demonic stuff at all. There is true evil out there and one has to know what they are getting into. It's not something to mess with. I don't hang out with convicts and criminals here on this plane so I am not interested investigating prisons or former mental facilities. They aren't places I would go to normally, so I would rather go to places where people had good times or to their homes where families shared their lives together. I enjoy that."

Michael, who was born in New York State, went to a home in Louisburg built in 1820. Seven others were with him, but he recorded a male voice who shouted, 'Get outttt!' His colleagues joked that maybe it was because he is from the north, a real, live Yankee.

THHS was invited to do the famous **Berry Hill Plantation** in South Boston, Virginia by GHOSTS of Raleigh. NC HAGS Paranormal Observers came along as well. This was part of a Halloween promotion with Audrey Dickerson of WLUS Radio in Oxford, North Carolina. She is a personality on the "Mike and Audrey's Most Music Morning Show."

William Byrd II was the original owner of the 105,000 acre land granted in 1728. Later Benjamin Harrison, the fourth Governor of Virginia and signer of the Declaration of Independence became an owner. Onetime owner, James Cole Bruce built the present Greek revival mansion in 1842. Some people have reported seeing his ghost on the property.

Presently the Berry Hill Plantation is an executive conference center and leisure resort. The property has whittled down to 750 acres.

On this excursion into the unknown, Michael, tapping his sense of humor, waved his hand and asked distinctly, "Can you see me wave?" Clear and loud came a "Yes!" and the EVP (electronic voice phenomena) was archived on video. The best EVP that night was found the next day as Michael reviewed his audio. In a southern female voice came 'Hi Michael' very loudly recorded.

He explains to me, "We use ITC devices as well. One is called the PX device that was created specifically for attracting voices from beyond the grave. The PX has a 2,048 word dictionary that purportedly changes when EMF readings spike. They require lithium batteries for strength."

As the investigators began leaving the Plantation, they turned and said, "Thank you for allowing us to pay our respects."

Michael went on to tell me about the **Country Squire Inn** of Warsaw, North Carolina and the charming Ms Iris Lennon, whose Scottish accent and heritage shines through. The restaurant was established in 1961 by Joe West, building it with aged logs and wood from antique structures. The present owner took over in 1993. She has since expanded to include a winery in the portion built in the 1700s and has added a Gift Shop and Tartan Tasting Room and more.

"I called the Inn and introduced myself as a paranormal investigator. The lady responded with 'would you like to come down and investigate?' Sure, I said. We all went down and had dinner. The woman showed us around. She said to lock up after we were finished or stay overnight if we liked. She stood at the door with me to show me how to lock up. I had my recorders with me. We investigated the whole night, but we didn't have any (noticeable) personal experiences. It was a tremendous place.

"When I got home, reviewing my recorders, there was an EVP of a little girl between us at the door, saying 'See hannahthistle, See hannahthistle.' That's what I got on the recorders. It's rare that we get a child. I thought to myself, but what the hell is a hannahthistle? I emailed my result to Ms Iris and asked what is a hannahthistle?

"Ms Iris called me the following day and was confused. She asked how the recorders worked. She then told me, 'We have a cat in the back yard and her name is Hannah Thistle.' I said, Oh Wow! That means the little ghost girl was trying to ask us if we saw the cat and possibly get our attention."

The Stagville Plantation in Durham, North Carolina was one of the largest pre-Civil War plantations in the South. At one time 900 slaves worked on 30,000 acres. The Bennehan family was the owner of that vast estate and the ca. 1700s Bennehan House and other structures on the property that includes the family cemetery.

The first owner of Stagville, Richard Bennehan helped to lay out the city of Raleigh. When he passed away in 1825, his holdings included one whole city block, Horton Grove and other plantations in three counties; Granville, Wake and Orange, part of which later became Durham County.

The Bennehan family left a legacy behind of their personal and business papers giving us a clear picture of life on a plantation before the War Between the States. Stagville is on the National Register of Historic Places. Ghosts and hauntings have been reported for decades by staff, neighbors and passers-by.

The Lake Lure Inn opened to receive guests in 1927. Many notables stayed there over the years, including President and Mrs. Franklin D. Roosevelt, F. Scott Fitzgerald, Emily Post, Calvin Coolidge, and actors from the *Dirty Dancing* 1987 movie cast. Much of the movie was filmed in Lake Lure including interior shots. In 1996 My Fellow Americans was filmed there as were scenes from *The Last of the Mohicans*.

Dr. Lucius Boardman Morse was a practicing physician in Illinois when he was diagnosed with tuberculosis. He came to the Chimney Rock area seeking a better climate, where he resided at the Cliff Dwellers Inn. He purchased property with the financial aid of his twin brothers Hiram and Asahel and created the dam that formed the lake. His wife, Elizabeth Parkinson is credited with naming the lake. The town of Lake Lure was incorporated in 1927 also. The fourth generation of their families still own and run the Chimney Rock Park.

The Lake Lure Inn was commissioned during World War II by the Army for recuperating military.

A few of the rooms on the third floor have been reported haunted. Apparitions have been seen in the dining room that is thought to be Dr. Morse. THHS captured an apparition photo in the main lobby.

The Battleship North Carolina, first of the Navy's modern warships, was launched on 13 June 1940. It guarded aircraft carriers serving in every major battle in the Pacific during World War II and only lost ten men during battle. She was decommissioned in 1947 and later placed on Inactive Reserve Fleet in New Jersey. In 1961 her destiny was the scrap yard until the citizens of North Carolina succeeded in bringing her home to Wilmington and dedicating her as a memorial to North Carolinians of all services killed in World War II.

It is said that two of the men killed in the war remain active with the ship.

THE HERITAGE HUNTERS SOCIETY (THHS)
Michael La Chiana, Founder and Field Investigator
John Brennan, Co-Founder/Field Investigator
Anne La Chiana, Case Manager/Field Investigator
Chris C. Finch, Field Investigator

Michael has enough knowledge, access to stories of his associates, friends and his own experiences to write a book of his own and plans to do that.

PART TWO: LEGENDS

Person's Ordinary Photo by Mark Forrest

Secrets in Person's Ordinary
(On the National Register of Historic Places)

This story came to me by way of Mark Forrest. He graciously gave me a thorough tour of Person's Ordinary in Littleton and the basic story to go with it. I followed up with research, research, research.

In Colonial times people of means that traveled usually stayed at a family or friends of a family's house, or even the house of a casual acquaintance with a 'letter of introduction' to compliment them. But those that traveled unaccepted in higher society had to opt for a stagecoach stop. These places were for the ordinary people; hence the name Ordinary came to be used.

Person's Ordinary is the last pre-Revolutionary Ordinary still standing in North Carolina. Thanks to the Littleton Woman's Club it has been restored and can be visited to get the feel of an earlier time in our country's history. Those who are sensitive to 'other worlds' may get the feel of it here .....or *see* even more.

Thomas Person was born in Brunswick County, Virginia. When he was about seven years old his father William moved the family across the border to Granville County, North Carolina where he became their first sheriff. Young Person studied surveying emerging as surveyor to Lord Granville. Quickly he learned to begin acquiring landed estates that eventually made him one of the largest land owners in North Carolina in the eighteenth century.

He emulated his father's footsteps by becoming sheriff but first he served as Justice of the Peace; later he represented Granville County in the North Carolina General Assembly in 1764. On 24 June 1765 he married Johannah Thomas also of Granville County. They had no children.

While becoming a famed politician and wealthy planter, he resided, sometimes in Personton (now Littleton) North Carolina and sometimes at his Granville County plantation. It is documented that he also helped many people by loaning money to them presumably to buy or maintain their farms or businesses.

Having good business sense and having traveled on the stagecoach road from Hillsborough up to his Bute County (now Littleton) plantation and east through to politically and commercially important

Halifax gave him an idea. The trip took two or three days to complete probably depending on the weather, road conditions, etc. The route was heavily traveled by stagecoach, horses, horse and wagons, and by foot. The long stretches between towns were sparsely occupied by residents. A day's travel was calculated at an average of seven miles. Person applied and was granted a lycense to keep an Ordinary on his property on 20 November 1764. It is believed that the building dates to 1739.

Entering the front door into the original portion of the house and looking to the right, shows a corner fireplace with a grand double-shoulder stone chimney which gives off warmth to the second story. Another corner fireplace sits in the back room where the stairs rise to the attic. It was probably Person who added an additional room on each level on the east side of the dwelling. This time installing a single-shoulder stone chimney with a brick stack for heating, thus providing more room for travelers to sleep 'tight' in their rope beds.

While Person split his time between his Granville Plantation and the Personton house, he most likely employed someone to actually run the business. Politics caught his attention and he was actively involved even as early as 1771 wanting freedom from oppressive England. Governor William Tryon ordered Person arrested and had him jailed as a Regulator conspirator in spite of his not being at the combat site during the Battle of Alamance in then-Orange County. Person's political power was recognized but no evidence was presented so he was released, remaining prominent in politics representing Granville County in the Provincial Congresses.

In 1776 Person sat on the committee of the Halifax Resolves which empowered delegates to enjoin other colonies in voting for independence from England at the Second Continental Congress. North Carolina was the first to instruct its delegates to the Continental Congress to vote for independence from the British. The Revolutionary War broke out as Person helped create the State Constitution of 1776.

He was appointed Brigadier General but again remained in the political arena.

During the Revolutionary War period North Carolina was busy freeing itself of Tories and the King's rule, especially west of the low country in the east that came to be called the Piedmont. The British armies and the Continentals both crossed North Carolina's soil. Person's Ordinary was busy with the comings and goings of travelers. It was located on the bustling roadway from Durham and Raleigh to the north. It is reported that British General Cornwallis stayed at the Ordinary, as did General Nathanael Greene as his Continental troops camped nearby.

Some of the journeymen sleeping overnight at the Ordinary were carrying orders and secret documents meant for the eyes of a general only. Wherever there is war there are spies and assassins.

Catastrophe happened one particular night in the wee hours before dawn. When the rest of the Ordinary had settled down for a good night of sleep and the surrounds were quiet, a fight broke out in the upstairs east sleeping room. The sound of metal clashed and clanked against each other. Boots stamped upon the floor as two men danced in fatal steps. Swords swashed, thrust forward and back. Grunts and accusations grew louder as the men fought. Then as quickly as it started, as fiercely as it was fought, the clashing ended. Silence hung heavy in the air. One man spread out on the floor obviously dying. His blood was soaking his clothes. The dark stain was spreading rapidly and ever wider, seeping deep across the floorboards. Another man, awake and watching the struggle hurriedly assisted the survivor.

"Hurry sir." He spoke quietly while helping him gather his things. "No one else must know you were here. Your horse and your men wait for you."

The duel was not recorded. The lives of men depended on secrecy. Silence from witnesses was extremely important. But an undeniable record remains. The would-be assassin's blood continues to stain the floorboards. The scrubbing, bleaching and sanding efforts have never removed the evidence of a duel fought during a passionate time of a struggle for freedom and liberty. No matter the efforts of man to remove the mark of a duel fought. The blood stains always rise to the surface of the floorboards as a reminder that there were two sides to this fight for liberty. The spirit of the assassin still waits lying in those dark stains upon the floor, waiting.......for reinforcements or assistance? We'll never know.

It is not written but it is rumored that the fleeing man was the Frenchman, Marquis de Lafayette.

The Marquis was in this area during the Revolutionary War. He arrived in South Carolina in 1777, a teenage nobleman, eager and schooled in military strategy. His brother-in-law general Louis Marie de Noailles was also committed to the cause of liberty, leading the bombardment of Savannah, Georgia in 1779. The men of the French army respected Lafayette and he soon gained the respect of General George Washington and of the patriotic colonial men fighting the war.

From South Carolina Lafayette proceeded to Philadelphia. He was closely associated with General Nathanael Greene commanding his respect even after Greene was thoroughly disgusted with other French generals. He was with Greene in the earlier part of the war in Rhode Island and the Chesapeake Bay areas. Washington eventually placed him in charge of the armies in Virginia.

It was commonly known that Lafayette would go off by himself without bodyguards to protect him. Enemies were also aware that his troops were encamped at Malvern Hill, Virginia near the North Carolina border.

The following advertisement appeared in the *Virginia Gazette* in 1779: 'Stolen from the subscriber in Warren County, near Thomas Person's Ordinary, a sorrel horse, etc. The thief has been seen with the above horse in his possession near the Butterwood Ordinary in Amelia County. Reward $100 etc. signed, Unity Coleman.'

Person's Ordinary continued serving its community after the American Revolution. The town changed its name from Personton to Littleton to honor the respected William Person Little, Thomas Person's sister May Ann's son. He had purchased the Ordinary and property from his mother's inheritance.

People of note continued to be guests of the Ordinary. Thomas Malone and Captain Edmund Pendleton stayed there along with Aaron Burr while escorting him from Bute County Courthouse to Richmond, Virginia to attend his trial for treason. Horace Greeley was known to have stayed there probably on his way to Warrenton to marry his lovely bride, Mary Youngs Chaney.

William Little housed the first Littleton post office. Students boarded at Person's during their attendance at nearby Little Manor School attributed to builder Thomas Bragg, Sr. It quartered Confederate troops during the War Between the States. While the Littleton Female College waited for their building to be finished, they used the Person's Ordinary building.

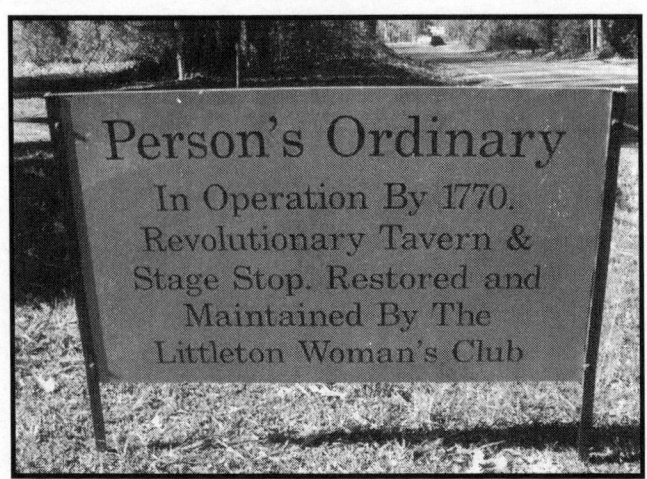

Person's Ordinary Sign From the Author's Collection

Author's Note: The ladies of the Littleton Woman's Club took on the project in 1956 of restoring and maintaining this most important reminder of our past history. Through grants and fund raisers they continue their efforts by opening the inn for tourists' visits and for use in community events. A scale model can also be seen in Littleton.

A Soldier's Impressions: The Braxton Bragg Story

The Bragg family in this country dates back to the Jamestown, Virginia colony ca. 1607. Thomas Bragg came from England with his brothers John and William, teenagers brought by ship under the command of Captain Christopher Newport. Thomas served in the English Navy and was rewarded with land in the new colony. He married Mary (Molly) the captain's daughter in 1615.

The Bragg line served as patriots in the Revolutionary War and some fought in the War of 1812. John's family lived in Carteret County before he moved them to Craven County, North Carolina where Braxton Bragg's father Thomas was born. As the young man grew his reputation boasted skill as a carpenter.

Thomas then moved to Warrenton, Warren County in 1800, probably from the New Bern area; married Margaret Crossland in 1803; became quite a successful carpenter and builder (work attributed to him still stands today) and acquired much land and property in his lifetime even extending into Alabama. He also owned a shop with ready-made building components which was quite unusual for the time.

Braxton's mother was the daughter of Alexander and Catharine Crossland who divorced three years before Braxton was born in 1817. Catharine Crossland lived just outside the town limits on The Crossland Place.

It has been written that young Braxton felt the sting of rejection from his peers. Perhaps this uncommon situation of divorced grandparents contributed to that feeling along with his being aware of his father being a craftsman rather than a gentleman. This may have reflected later in the treatment of his subordinates with cold disdain and rigid adherence of military propriety. Sometimes this was referred to being carried to the point of absurdity. This aloofness probably also contributed to his ability to turn raw recruits into disciplined soldiers.

Thomas and Margaret Bragg provided good education for their offspring. Their children fared well in their time. John served as a judge and a U. S. Congressman from Alabama; Thomas, Jr. served as a U.S. senator and as governor of North Carolina from 1855 to 1859; Alexander became a respected builder in North Carolina and Alabama; Braxton distinguished himself in the military and became a General in the Confederate Army; Dunbar was a merchant, a postmaster and later a judge in Freestone County, Texas; William died in battle fighting for the Confederacy in the War Between the States. The daughters were: Margaret, Catherine, Elizabeth, Mary and Sarah.

Braxton graduated from the Warrenton Male Academy then proceeded to graduate in the top five in his class at U.S. Military Academy at West Point. He fought successfully in the Second Seminole War in Florida. In the Mexican War he earned promotions and won respect for his bravery fighting under General Zachary Taylor with Jefferson Davis. Many of the military leaders on both sides of the American Civil War had fought as junior officers in Mexico, including Ulysses S. Grant, George B. McClellan, Ambrose Burnside, Stonewall Jackson, James Longstreet, George Meade, and Robert E. Lee, as well as the future Confederate President Jefferson Davis.

The presence of a large number of graduates from the United States Military Academy worked in favor of the U.S. Army. These officers, mostly lieutenants and captains, formed a tight knit corps whose leadership ability and training helped offset the initial shortage of manpower. Historians point out that their ranks included men such as George G. Meade, **Ulysses S. Grant**, George B. McClellan, P.G.T. Beauregard, Braxton Bragg, Joseph E. Johnston, and Robert E. Lee, officers who later went on to command the great armies of the War Between The States.

Between wars he met, fell in love and married Elisa Brooks Ellis on 7 June 1849, the daughter of the wealthy Louisiana owner of

Evergreen Plantation in Terrebonne Parish. After serving the U.S. Army for nineteen years, he retired to become a successful sugar planter in Thibodaux, Louisiana where he designed a levee and drainage system for the state.

As states began to secede he jumped into action in organizing the Louisiana military board. He quickly became major general of the newly formed Louisiana State Army. As the War escalated, Confederate President Jefferson Davis appointed him Brigadier General during the Civil War. His skill in organization showed when he reduced corruption and improved the supply system. Credit goes to him for refining the conscription process and chain of command within the ranks.

The Union seized his plantation property in 1862. Bragg and his wife were both arrested at the close of the War but they were immediately released. He went on to serve as a Civil Engineer for improving the harbor in Mobile Bay, Alabama. Next he migrated to Galveston, Texas where he held the position of Chief Engineer for the Gulf, Colorado and Santa Fe Railway newly chartered in 1873. He formulated plans for its construction.

In 1876 Bragg was walking down a street in Galveston with a friend when he collapsed and died. His body is buried in Mobile, Alabama. Ft. Bragg in North Carolina is one of many places named after Braxton Bragg.

The Gulf, Colorado and Santa Fe Railroad ran a line through the Big Thicket (later it became a forest preserve) in Hardin County, Texas connecting Saratoga to an area full of oil and lumber in the early 1900s. A small town grew up around the railroad depot named Bragg (a station, then a town) honoring the memory of the man they respected. The site eventually played out; the railroad dismantled the train track leaving a seven-mile-long dirt road called Bragg Road.

The road is thickly forested on both sides with some areas covered over with a canopy of trees nearly forming a natural tunnel. At night it is the darkest of darks. Bragg Road has become known as a Ghost Road because of the haunting activities. It is sometimes call the Bragg Light.

Reports of this light being seen go back to the days when the train traveled the track. But it was after the removal of the track in 1934 that the activity increased. Hundreds of people flocked to Bragg Road to see the light for themselves. Paranormal investigators came with their high-tech equipment to record the ghosts that haunt the road.

For thirty years the commissioners of Hardin County have wanted to cut the timber on Bragg Road to add a possible $100,000 to the county purse. The residents object to changing anything on Bragg Road. They want it kept natural even with reports of a glowing ball of light dancing through the trees. They state that prestigious National Geographic has featured a picture of the road in their October 1978 magazine showing the light down the road. Japanese TV has also chosen to show the phenomena publicly.

Ghost Hunters drive down the road at night taking photos that show active orbs and lots of movement. Orbs in various colors and sizes appear. Unexplained light shadowy figures show up in photographs taken in pure darkness. Some seekers have experienced unexplained sensations and of movement of their truck while they are sitting in a stopped position.

Many theories float around from one person to another; Mexicans who laid the track, but instead of getting paid, were murdered and buried roadside; a decapitated man with a lantern; mystic phenomena where Spanish conquistadores have buried treasure; a Jayhawker shot by Confederates; a night hunter who got lost in the woods. I'm sure there are more.

But I wonder if an unsettled General Braxton Bragg is on the job, his last position of a turbulent life and career, just doing his best as he had always done.

PART THREE: TALES BROUGHT TO LAKE GASTON

Lake Gaston is an approximately 35-mile long lake with 350 miles of shoreline, maximum width of 1.3 miles, and maximum depth of 95 feet. It was forged from the Roanoke River in1963 by the Virginia Electric Power Company building the Gaston Dam to generate hydro-electric power. Dominion Resources owns the lake and created it to include flood control and recreation purposes.

The name Lake Gaston honors the memory of the esteemed William J. Gaston (1778-1844) who was a lawyer, senator, congressman, and jurist. He composed the song "The Old North State" which was adopted as the state song in 1927.

The Roanoke River (called the Staunton River in Virginia) was the main transportation and supply route for Native Americans and the early settlers coming into the area as early as mid-1600s. It runs from the eastern Appalachian-Blue Ridge Mountains in the west, across the Piedmont to the Albemarle Sound in the east.

Kerr Lake Reservoir feeds Lake Gaston which feeds Roanoke Rapids. Lake Gaston and Kerr Lake are popular areas with a rural feel to it, yet have easy access to I-95 and I-85.

The north shore of Lake Gaston mostly flows onto Virginia and the south shore ripples onto North Carolina. The stories in this section have been brought here by the folks who have settled around the lake. Word got around that I collect and write stories of hauntings. So it seemed that each time I attended a social gathering out at the Lake, I met someone with a tale to tell me. They came from many different areas of the country for different reasons. Their one commonality is that they love the sparkling lake, the tall forests that frame it and all the pleasures they give.

People and Their Ghosts: The Ann Herbert Stories

"I was about twelve years old the first time I remember having my first psychic experience. We lived in Maryland. Our landlord, Mr. Smith lived in an old colonial home. The basement had slave quarters in it.

"One day I was cleaning Mr. Smith's upstairs guest bedroom as his daughter was expected to come for a visit. His dog, a friendly collie I was familiar with, was sprawled on the rug in the middle of the room. As I cleaned he stood up, slowly moving toward me growling. Alarmed, I backed out onto the balcony outside the open door. I paused there a few minutes. When the collie settled down I came back into the room and finished cleaning. He never did that again and I wasn't aware of him ever doing that before. I know he saw something in that room that I didn't see. Apparently he scared it away because I had no problem after that. Maybe he was even protecting me. I'm not sure.

"In later years Mr. Smith closed off most of the house and just lived in a certain portion of it. My brother Don was there one day visiting with, by now an elderly Mr. Smith, when a rocking chair in the corner of the room started rocking. No one else was in the room. The room was closed off with no open windows or doors to create wind movement. My brother's face is very expressive. Mr. Smith must have noticed the change of expression.

"He just piped up looking my brother straight in the eye. 'Oh, don't bother about him.'

To not be alarmed by the rocking movement Mr. Smith must have seen these occurrences often. He probably lived with many *other people* in the house. It's a house so full of past history."

Ann contacted her sister Donna about any of her thoughts on Mr. Smith's house. She mentioned a cage in the attic supposedly where a madwoman was once kept. When Ann told her brother Don about it he added his own experiences.

"My brother Don has memories of his own. He recently told me, 'I remember seeing a cage-like-thing of wooden slats in the attic when Dad and I were helping Mr. Smith clean it out in preparation to move away. That was the day he, Dad, and Mr. Smith were in the living room talking when a door to the room slammed shut by itself so hard that their ears were ringing.'

"Mr. Smith had gone out somewhere one night when my brother was alone in the house. He was upstairs painting one of the bedrooms. There was a constant loud roaring sound, like wind blowing, but there was no wind. He kept painting then poof, the sound stopped. All of a sudden, the door to the room opened and Mr. Smith's collie walked in. He left the house quickly and never went in there at night again. Dog or no dog, he was gone! He had never been scared like that before.

"My brother and I talked about Mr. Smith's house discussing the things we knew happened there, in particular the doctor's story. When we picked strawberries in Mr. Smith's fields in the summer we always stopped to read a doctor's headstone where he was buried right in the middle of the field. The doctor hanged himself in one of Mr. Smith's upstairs bedrooms. We don't know any more than that but surmised he must have been an extremely unhappy man, enough to hold his spirit to this place maybe."

***

Ann continued with stories of other *happenings* to her in other places and times.

"When I was a young married, still a girl really in 1976 I moved with my husband to Milo, Piscataquis County, Maine. We rented a place in an old house that was divided into upstairs and downstairs apartments. Ours was downstairs. In our bedroom I sensed something in our closet, nothing other than a sense. But I wouldn't go in my bedroom if my husband wasn't home. That's how strong my senses were raised and the alarm it instilled in me.

"After a while I began talking to a girl who grew up there. I told her about my senses and that closet. She told me a sixteen-year-old boy that lived in my apartment was hit by a car and killed right in front of the house. I still never went into that bedroom if I was home alone. I moved back home, alone, to Maryland in less than two years."

Author's Note: The town of Milo was named after a famous athlete, Milo of Croton, in Ancient Greece. The town sits where the Sebec and Piscataquis Rivers converge, in the very center of Maine. Actually the Methodist Church there is the dead center. Benjamin Sargent and his son Theophilus settled there in 1802 beginning a trading center. Trafton's Falls provided water power for the early industry. Soon Milo sported a gristmill, produced lumber products, and a woolen textile mill ran successfully until it burned down in the 1840s. Later the American Thread Company located a factory there.

Ann continued: "Still living in Maryland, I remarried. Then I had quite different experiences. I'd wake up in the middle of the night out of a deep sleep to see a young black man standing alongside of the bed looking down at me. He wasn't threatening me, just looking down at me. One time I nudged my husband awake.

"I said calmly but forcefully, 'Mike, there's a man standing next to the bed.' He woke with fists flying in the air. Getting up he continued swinging his arms and hands in the air. Then he went for his gun, walked all through the house to find nothing at all. Of course he didn't. The man just, poof, disappeared. This happened several times. Mike had a very bad temper. After talking with his previous wife and seeing the bruises she still carried, I left the marriage.

"Then I met Gary. We were together for a few years living in a different house and a different town but still in Maryland when the same experience happened. I woke from a deep sleep.

"I nudged Gary to say, 'There's a man standing here.' He reached over in a comforting manner, patting me. 'It's okay. Just go back to sleep,' he said in a calm way. It never happened again. I firmly believe the young man was my guardian angel protecting me. Finally, I didn't need him right alongside of me anymore."

***

As we sat and talked about paranormal and psychic phenomena Ann filled me in on psychic abilities evident in other members of her family.

"My daughter moved into my parents' house to help take care of my mom when she became ill. In time Mom passed away and my dad had gone into the hospital battling cancer. My daughter came home from work, ran in to take a shower before running out to meet friends. When she came out of the shower, the TV was playing with no one there to turn it on, and she *saw* Mom at the kitchen sink. It was ice-cold in that spot now where Mom always stood when she was alive. When I think of Mom, that's where I picture her.

"But my daughter said, 'Grandmom, you're scaring me.' That was the end of it. She came back no more. My brother experienced psychic ability in Mr. Smith's house and also after my mother passed away. She came into his room just one time. I think it was a farewell visit.

"My son Bob had an unusual experience when he was in West Virginia. He was driving his car uphill when he slipped the car into neutral. The car continued up the hill! He then turned the car around, heading down the same hill and this time when he placed the car in neutral the car was *pushed* up the hill in reverse! I have no idea what that was all about, only that it happened."

***

The next experience didn't really happen to Ann but she was a party to it.

"Our neighbors Bill and Ruth were the first to place a house, in the mid 1980s, in this Lake Gaston area where we live. They were in their late 60s or early 70s when we first moved here in 1995. We only knew them a couple of years before Ruth died on the day after Thanksgiving. Prior to Thanksgiving Day that year she came over to give me a hand-crocheted baby blanket for my recently born granddaughter.

"She started talking about being depressed and why Bill was against having a Will or updating the one they had, I'm not sure which it was. She decided that she was going to take care of their funeral arrangements when they went up to New Jersey at Christmas time.

"The evening after Thanksgiving she was sitting in her favorite chair, had a sudden pain, slipped to the floor and died. She never got a chance to make those arrangements that concerned her so much. Later I found out that she had already had an aneurysm. That's probably the cause of her death.

"We weren't here that day. Bill called Doris (she also lives in our little community) because she is a nurse. Of course they took her to the hospital to try to revive her anyway, as they usually do. Bill remained in the house for a while before his worsening health caused him to move to his daughter's house in Clarksville. He came here some of the time but the majority of the time he would be at his daughter Tracy's home. He passed away a few years after his wife died.

"The house remained empty during this time. Daughters Tracy and Jill tried to use it as a weekly or monthly vacation rental. That didn't work out to well. Then a couple from Buffalo, New York came down to rent it for the winter months. They arrived here on Thanksgiving Day. They stayed until around April or May. I remember their names as Don and Bonnie. One day Bonnie saw me outside and came over. She spoke quietly with a questioning look on her face as she said, 'I want to ask you something but I don't want you to think I'm nosy.' As she was indicating Miss Ruth's home she asked me if anyone died in the house.

"I replied yes. And she told me, 'She's still there, mostly in the master bedroom. We just don't sleep in the master bedroom because she's still there.' She repeated herself as if to punctuate her statement. She didn't say much more than that and I didn't want to probe.

"In 2005 another couple rented the house for over a year while their singlewide trailer was being replaced by a modular at Kerr Lake. They stayed here while the work was being done. I didn't say a word to them about the previous tenants' experience with Miss Ruth.

"One day I was down at the dock with my son Mark. The neighbor walked over and asked me if I knew if there were any boogers in the house. She was indicating Miss Ruth's house. We started laughing because the term she used was unfamiliar to us.

"She said, rather excitedly, that there *were* boogers in that house! She went on to say things were a bit crazy in the house telling us that she would be cooking and the stove would turn on high with no hand turning the knob. Someone was rattling the silverware drawer in the middle of the night. One night she woke up and felt hair being dragged across her face. There was a doll in the house that had long hair. She believed it was the doll's hair that she felt crossing her face. Then she somehow realized her son was in trouble. Their eight-year-old son was a diabetic. His blood sugar was dangerously low.

"It was only then I told her about the former tenant. She then told me that she would not sleep in the master bedroom either. She shared her son's room. Her husband sleeps there. One day he was taking an afternoon nap. She heard him yelling, stop shaking the bed. Stop it! She went in to see what all the commotion was about. She quickly let him know she had been in the kitchen. It wasn't her.

"I thought about these happenings for a while and consulted my friend Heidi. We concluded that many of Miss Ruth's personal items were still in the house including her Bible. It seemed to us that Miss Ruth wasn't happy with strangers handling her personal things. We gathered her personal items, placed them in a box and Heidi took them home to later give to the daughter. The family moved away and into their new home as planned.

"A new tenant moved into the house. He never *sees*, *senses* or *experiences* anything out of the ordinary. Peace has settled into Miss Ruth's home".

Spirit Doesn't Know She is Dead: Heidi's Story

When I was about 12 years old my parents bought a house in Cedar Knolls, New Jersey. My mother was working for a Realtor and found a house that just came onto the market. We moved from Morristown over to this house that had been empty for two years. It was small by today's standards. It had a kitchen, an arched formal dining room, another arch going into the living room, three bedrooms and bath, of course. I remember the woodwork was exquisite, all natural chestnut wood trim and wood floors. It also had an attic and huge basement.

Some months after we settled in I had surgery resulting from polio on my legs. So I was tucked into a hospital bed set up in the dining room for three months. After healing I finally went back to school. We were living in the house about eight months by then and my mother went into the attic to clean it out. She wanted my father to build two bedrooms up there so my sister and I could each have our own room. My sister was two years older than me and we got into each other's way as young teenagers do.

But the basement was the first job tackled by my father, a carpenter by trade. He worked all day for a contractor, came home to dinner, and then went down into the basement. Many nights I joined him just sitting on a stool to watch. Dad and I were very close.

He separated the cellar, building a recreation room on one side and a workshop room with a door for himself. He put up workbenches, hung his carpentry tools, lined his walls with shelves placing all his coffee cans full of different size nails, screws and all those odds and ends carpenters collect certain they'll need them later.

While Dad was in the cellar, Mom was in the attic. It was loaded with all kinds of stuff including ten bibles of different sizes and age. Some had clippings of hair or dried flowers inside. They contained information on different branches of the family. One bible was huge, over 100 years old and about 16" X 24." My mother found a bamboo table, took that big bible and placed it on top and put in her bedroom. There were also knitting needles and supplies, materials, boxes and boxes of clothing, blankets and stuff people just stick into the attic to deal with later.

Knowing it had taken the son two years to settle the estate and to clean the house of items he wanted to take with him, Mom called him. She told him of all the stuff she found including the bibles, coins and dollar bills. He came and took a box with him, telling her, "Whatever else you find, I don't want it. Just toss it." She gave the bibles to the neighbor that had known the woman and to the church.

The son's mother was Mrs. Losey. She was widowed and lived alone in the house. One morning she fell down the cellar steps, injured and unable to get help, she died there. Her son found her when he stopped in to check on her.

Sometime after all this household activity began my brother and I were in the living room watching TV. All of a sudden we heard a racket of doors opening and closing banging in an angry way. Drawers were opening and closing loudly like someone was frantically searching through the dressers and mad because they couldn't find what they were looking for. It was loud and it was coming from the upstairs bedroom. This went on for quite a while.

Finally I said to Billy, "What the heck is Audrey looking for?" I was talking about my sister.

With that knowing look on his face he replied, "I don't know. You know how she is when she starts looking for something."

"Do you think I should go up and say something?'

"No! Don't. Leave her alone. Okay?"

This went on for at least ten minutes. We could hear her move from one room to another bumping and clunking. It was obvious where the noises were coming from. All of a sudden it stopped.

"See, I told you she'd stop."

With that said, we finished watching our program. A half hour later my sister and mother walked in through the back door. We looked at each other with eyes as wide as could be! Looking at my sister we both asked, "Where were you?"

"At the neighbors with Mom. Why?"

We told them what happened.

"I'm not going upstairs!"

"I'm not going upstairs either!" Billy piped in.

"Don't be ridiculous." Mom said as she headed for the stairs. When she came back down, "There's nobody there. Nothing is disturbed. No drawers are open. Everything is as it should be."

There had been no one else in the house but Billy and me.

Soon after that incident Mom started missing things. A beautiful pair of glass candlesticks, an anniversary gift, had gone missing. They were always kept in the china closet. We looked everywhere for them. We could not find them.

Then there was a knife from the kitchen that Mom used every day. It was gone. Just gone. Even when we closed up and cleaned out the house after Mom and Dad passed away, we never found that knife.

For a time we had all our boxed games on the attic stairs. They were piled there, games with tiles, little plastic pieces, paper money and marbles inside the boxes.

Mom constantly told us, "When you go upstairs, carry those games up and put them on the shelf where they belong. If you don't, one of these days they're gonna all get knocked down and it's gonna be a mess."

One day we sat down to eat dinner. We're all there, my mother, father, sister, brother, and me. All of a sudden we heard every one of those games fall down the steps and hit the attic door. We heard the marbles roll, the tiles tinkling, the little plastic thingys; all of them hit the door.

"I told you, I told you! Now all three of you go up and pick up those things right now!"

We dragged ourselves away from the table, heads down, guilty expressions. We opened the attic door. Not a thing was disturbed! The boxes were piled just as we left them!

Footsteps were heard from time to time. We got used to them and just ignored them. They were harmless.

A month or so later, it happened again. My mother, father, brother and I were getting ready again to sit down for dinner. My sister was at her girlfriend's house. We heard the crash, this time from Father's workshop in the basement. It sounded like every nail, every screw every bit of metal crashing to the floor! The whole shelf must have come down!

Mom started, "I told you, I told you! You have too much stuff on those shelves! I told you, it's too heavy for those shelves. We have other things to do and now we have to go down and clean up your mess!"

"Don't worry. I'll clean it up."

Of course I piped in willing to help, too. We went down to the cellar and not one can was out of place. Not one thing. It was the freakiest thing! So we went back up to tell Mom.

"Don't tell me that! I heard it!"

We reassured her, it was the truth. Not a thing out of place.

Then she said, "Evidently Mrs. Losey is looking for something."

After that, Mom must have sought out someone for advice. The next time she heard noises upstairs when no one was there, she went up and confronted Mrs. Losey.

"Let me help you find what you're looking for, I gave everything to your son. The big bible is in my bedroom, you can look at it there………."

Mrs. Losey's activity got less and less. On occasion the door to my father's workshop opened and closed on its own when we were in the 'rec' room. Our friends were there and witnessed that. We laughed saying to our friends, "you can come over but Mrs. Losey's here." They ran out and wouldn't come back into the house again.

Eventually it faded completely. Until then my brother, sister and I were afraid to stay in the house alone. We knew she wouldn't hurt us but it was too freaky.

***

My mother died only four years after Pete and I married. I always loved the set of dishes that she bought when I was little. She kept them in the china closet along with a lot of cut glass brought from Germany.

"Well, you can have the dishes when I die and your sister can have the cut glass."

And that's how it was after she passed away. I kept the dishes packed in a box while we lived in our apartment in Madison, New Jersey. Our three children were born there. We worked hard and struggled to buy an old house in the countryside of Port Norris. The house was in the woods.

Since Pete worked a half hour away and we had only one car, I was pretty much stranded up there with the boys. So whenever Pete was working I brought Bullet, the German Shepherd dog he gifted me during our first year of marriage, into the house with me. He grew to be a big, but sweet dog. When Pete was home the dog stayed outside. When Pete was working, Bullet came inside. Always.

One night after the boys were in bed I decided it was a good time to unpack my cherished dishes now that I had a place to put them. I brought out the box, opened it and started to unpack them on the floor in front of the china closet. The phone rang. Bullet was on the floor while I was talking, quite a while actually. Then his head popped up, he stood and a low rumble started in his chest. Grrrrrr. He growled but quietly under his breath. I immediately sensed the presence of my mother.

    The same thing happened when my father died. He had emphysema, contracted pneumonia and was bedridden in the hospital then passed away. I got a phone call from my brother telling me the sad news. I went upstairs to say a prayer. That's when I smelled his aroma. There was no doubt. He was there with me. I knew immediately that he came to say good-bye.

The Hobo and the Depression: Lynne's Stories

As a child I found it hard to believe in heaven. It just didn't make sense to me that people would be up in the sky as heaven was explained to me. It was more logical to me that people occupied our own space but in another dimension. Crowded, but it made more sense to me.

I'm from an old colonial town in upstate New York where my grandparents and generations before them, lived in a large old 1841 farmhouse. We often felt the presence of *other people* from other lifetimes living in the house. They didn't bother anyone so we didn't bother them. It was a very comfortable arrangement for all.

My grandparents were generous with sharing what they had to give. During the depression they often gave food to those who came to the door, including a particular hobo. This hobo carried a stick over his shoulder with his bundle tied to the end of it. He came more than once.

When I reached thirteen years old and attending high school my grandfather lay dying of leukemia. A bedroom was made up for him in the downstairs front parlor. All of our relatives passed their last hours at home where other family members took care of them. I was named after my grandfather but was called 'Little Lynne' to separate us. As I sat next to his bed holding his hand he was having vivid dreams more vivid than real life. They're called the dreams of the dead. I listened and talked to him about them.

Several years later I went off to Cornell University. My grandmother was still living in the house, which was set five houses up the street from ours. Every morning my mother went to Grandma's to open up the house, make her breakfast, spend the morning with her, and then see that she settled down for a nap in the afternoon. She went home returning later to make Grandma's dinner leaving her to watch television or whatever.

Grandma began thinking that Grandfather had given the hobo a key. She believed he was in the house and was becoming a bit obsessive about that particular man from the depression years. She was adamant about the doors being locked, asking explicitly, "Are all the doors locked?" and again, "Are you sure all the doors are locked?" We didn't realize how afraid she really was about that hobo.

When I came home during a break from Cornell University I stayed in the house with grandma while my parents were away. By now she was 86 years old with her bedroom downstairs.

When it was time to go to bed she said to me, "Lynne, would you lie down on my bed?"

"Why do you want me to lie down there?"

"Look, look here."

When I looked there was an imprint like a person's body on the bed.

"I'll be upstairs, Grandma, where I always sleep." With the *other people* is what I was thinking. I was familiar with them.

When she woke up from her nap she would throw a sweater into the parlor for Emma who was cold. By this time my mother thought she was having difficulty separating the people in her dreams at naptime incorporating them into her reality. She thought the people in her dreams were still in her parlor.

The old house had a back hallway that led to a place where you leave your boots and outdoor clothes. It eventually leads to a pretty backyard. To go from the kitchen to the TV room you had to walk through this hallway. This is where Grandma was afraid the hobo was hiding. We checked and reassured her that he wasn't there. No one was there.

My mother went up one morning after a freshly fallen snow lay heavy on the ground. She couldn't get into the house. It was locked up tight. She got my father to break in. Grandma was in the back hallway area on the floor up against the door. She had thrown the bolt on the door. It was still bolted. A huge oak table was overturned in the kitchen. The refrigerator door was open and a gallon of milk spilled on the floor. Obviously a terrible struggle had taken place. Grandma was passed out. She had a stroke.

There were no footprints anywhere around the house.

She had constant attention after that. I went up to sit with her as I did with Grandpa. It took some time before she began to talk. Eventually I got the story in bits and pieces that she had a fight with the hobo. She didn't live a long time after that. But the last time I saw her, as I was leaving she shouted out in a perfectly clear, young voice, "Good-bye Lynne. I love you!" I was never sure whether she was calling to Grandpa or to me.

So we always had these *other people* in the house. They were all gentle except for the one. The hobo.

Shrine of El Cristo Negro

We went with friends to see El Cristo Negro in Esquipulas, southeastern Guatemala near the El Salvador and Honduras border when my husband and I lived in South America. This is the most important shrine in Catholic Central America.

The Spanish Conquistadors commissioned the Black Christ to be sculpted in 1594 and then placed it in the local church in 1595. The site is believed to be sacred by the Mayans before the Spanish friars came building the four-domed basilica at the base of the small hill in 1758. The earlier church was nearby. The El Cristo Negro is carved from a dark balsa wood.

The pilgrimages can climb to as many as 10,000 people in a line moving slowly in the week prior to January 15 and again during Easter week. During these times the hotels and restaurants fill to overflowing.

As often happens in Latin America, the town surrounding the basilica is poor.

One of our friends was a diplomat so bodyguards escorted us. A protective car drove in front of ours and one followed behind us. A few in the group laughed because the church is known for its miracles. I felt it wrong to laugh and defended the people who came so far to be healed. Such faith and belief shouldn't be mocked. Plus there are testimonials throughout the village of people who have been healed. Busloads of people came all the time. People crawled on their knees passed concrete barriers to get inside.

My eyes were taking everything in, looking to capture as much as I could. I saw a pretty bride to the side on the steps with white flowers around her. I thought how fortunate for her to marry in such a spiritual place. As I walked into the church a huge amount of energy like "whoosh" swirled at me. Then this deep voice spoke to me, "I'm really here."

Whew! I felt knocked backwards. We were still 200 feet before reaching the altar. I felt this tremendous energy as we approached closer and closer up the corridor. I became silent. I didn't want to speak.

Then someone whispered that we could take the path to the side and go behind the Cristo Negro to worship. Now the ones in my group were touching me, saying "Pray for me Lynne. Ask for my shoulder to be healed. Pray for me Lynne." But I didn't feel anything sacred from the Cristo Negro. It was just a statue to me. We walked backwards as requested until we were out of the church. All this time the energy stayed with me until we reached the gift shop. I bought some crosses for my son, daughter and sister.

As we left we stopped on top of the hill to look down on the plaza and the church. I turned to my devout Catholic friend Marilyn, "Did you feel that?" I spoke softly to her. She looked at me in amazement replying to me. "No. I didn't feel anything. Oh, you are so lucky."

I didn't say anything else. My husband Paul, who is pretty much a non-believer, said he felt the energy.

When we reached our hotel a beautiful little boy was selling stuff. That's just the norm here. He held a necklace out to me.

"This is for you."

I looked down. "I don't have one cent in Honduran money or Guatemalan money. Not even one cent. But see that woman over there. She will buy it from you."

He replied to me. "No, I have to give it to you."

The boy was glowing. But I just couldn't accept it.

We went out that night for dinner and he followed us when we were returning to the hotel. My friends kept saying, "There's your little boy, there's your little boy." I said nothing. The next day we went out to see the famous ruins, Copan. I felt sad when I didn't see him around. But as we were leaving the area ending our visit he again appeared. "I have to give it to you." He said. So I took it handing him some money this time. "No, this is for you." Again he repeated, "This is for you." I took the necklace telling him that the money was a gift for his mother making it clear that I wasn't paying for the necklace." Finally he accepted the money.

Sometime later after my mother passed away, my brother and his wife were having a difference of opinion about the settlement of her home. I had gone out behind the house where her ashes were spread into the garden. I was furious, banging down my hand.

"Do something!" I shouted to no one there. I heard that same man's deep voice that I heard in the Church of the Cristo Negro.

"What will be will be."

My mother or anyone in my family would never have spoken these words. One other time when I went up to my mother's house, the same voice said, "I'm here."

Son

Our son Doug died suddenly at twenty-eight years old. He was in his last year of clinic, studying to become a chiropractor after receiving his bachelor's degree and going into medical school. He and his dog moved into his new apartment a few days before. One night as he was laying on the couch watching television he just quietly had a heart attack. When he didn't show up at work the next morning his neighbor hollered through the open door "Hey, you didn't go in to work this morning." Then he realized something was wrong, went in and found him.

When we drove down my husband Paul took my sister and brother-in-law to a motel. So I was alone in the apartment at the time. I said in desperation, "God, give me a sign. What happened? What happened?"

Just the week before my sister and I planned to come down in the next few days to decorate his apartment for him, so at this point the bed was not set together yet. At one o'clock that morning I lay wide-awake on his mattress on the floor. I felt a brush of a kiss on my cheek, European style followed by *a feeling* across my heart. It was slight but I thought it was a sign of love. The next day was the autopsy. I insisted that I see him before the autopsy.

At home we held a memorial service. We tried to keep it fairly private, for family. Yet when people heard about it they came from great distances, even from other countries where we'd lived. His college friends gave eulogies.

My grandchildren were here; they were about three and four and a half years old. Jennie took a rose and threw it into the water. The next day Zack, the older child woke up and hurried down to the lake. He was looking for the rose, hoping it would not wash back up on the shore. "Oh, Uncle Doug got the rose," he said.

He wanted to do something so I suggested he water the flowers. When I went down to check on him, he was happily shooting the hose up into the air.

"What are you doing?'

"Uncle Doug is thirsty." He was always conscious of Uncle Doug being around.

They went home. When they came back again Zack came rushing into the house. Then I heard him say, "I'm fine."

"What's that?" I asked him.

He then said "Well, Jackson (Doug's dog) said 'I'm so happy you're here' in this deep voice."

I wasn't alarmed or surprised because after Doug died I had running conversations with him. I'd walk up to the road with all these questions in my mind. 'Like what should we do about such and such a thing.' Immediately an answer would come to me and I knew it was from Doug. They were logistic questions with answers coming right back to me.

I had many vibrant dreams right after he died. I wondered if Doug was coming to me through my dreams. One such dream took place on the terrace outside our former house in Ecuador. The bright sun was gleaming down. The scene was beautiful. I turned the corner of the house and Doug was sitting at his desk.

"What are you doing?"

"Studying."

Next I asked "How do you like it so far?"

He replied to me, "It is okay, Mom."

"Made any friends yet?"

"Not really."

I had the distinct feeling that he had to study here in order to get there, to where he was in this beautiful place.

Then he said, "Could you get me a cell phone?"

Another dream I had was also placed in a house we lived in, my daughter was with me. My granddaughter was hiding in the closet. I got her out of the closet and Doug was standing there in his physical presence. I went to hug him and paused, he was stiff. He said, "Put your arms around me. I hugged him, feeling his muscular chest and his heart beating beneath it. Then he disappeared.

I've really talked to him more than seen him. I have running conversations with him all the time.

We've always communed with nature. Here we've watched an eagle fly and nest. After Doug passed we saw several eagles. One would fly toward us before turning and flying away. We often thought it was Doug appearing as an eagle or sending a sign to us. When Paul went down to the water for the first time to go onto his new boat, an eagle flew right toward him. Normally eagles don't do that.

My daughter, her husband and kids came down to our house in the summer after Doug had *passed over* that spring. We were all on the dock when an eagle soared down to within ten feet of us, scooped up a fish and flew off.

That same first summer after Doug died; my husband and I went with friends to Rome. Before we left I heard this voice say to me, 'take me with you.' I'd been worried that my *seeing* him studying meant that maybe he was in purgatory or something. I asked Sister Margaret about it and she replied, "No, that's normal. It's like a staging area."

We went into St. Peter's Basilica. It was the year of the Jubilee, 2000. The Jubilee is every 70 years I believe. Catholics are supposed to go through the portal of the main basilica once in their lifetime. We went but I wasn't Catholic at that time. There were thousands of people. I noticed some in groups wearing bright yellow tee shirts or something similar like that, so they wouldn't lose each other. All different nationalities came from all over on this hot day in June. Masses of people were moving together some humming, moving up to go through this portal. It was a very emotional scene to be part of that.

We moved up and through the portal, walking around. Paul and I were separated. I walked over to see Michelangelo's Pieta. That's when I saw this brilliant light coming out of this window right to me. I walked up towards the small area at the front of the church and the big window, going toward that light.

A mass was being held for the local people, not for tourists. I approached the priest and said in Spanish, "I need to take the missa." He hesitated ready to say no, but seeing the expression on my face, he allowed me into the line. People were moving up to receive the host of communion. I looked up toward that brilliant light, murmuring, 'Doug, I hope you are in the light.'

His voice, just as loud as could be replied, "I am, Mom!" It was clear as crystal. The priest paused as I reached for the host. I knew he felt it or heard it too.

A year and three months after Doug died, I needed a pacemaker implanted. They told me it is a simple operation (before showing me a nasty film about the operation. Ugh.) I was waiting quite a while in the hallway because the person ahead of me was taking longer than expected. I wonder if I passed over briefly during the operation. I saw ten men dressed in black suits lined up. Doug was in the middle.

"Mom!" he called out.

When I came awake after the operation the only thing I remembered is that I saw Doug.

Two months later during my scheduled mammogram I got talking with the technician.

"Please don't squeeze too hard, I have a new pacemaker."

She said, "Oh, I know all about pacemakers. When I started nursing I was in the operating room for some time."

"Really. Just how risky is that operation? I feel like I passed over while under the anesthesia."

"Oh yea. You definitely could've. You're on artificial support system during the operation. You could easily have technically died and been revived."

This past spring my daughter was sleeping in the upstairs bedroom. When she awoke, Doug was there. She said it creeped her out. She is very practical and not receptive to anything like psychic phenomena. We're all different.

It's funny. I've become so comfortable with knowing Doug is there. When I drive up through Pennsylvania toward my hometown, I'll say "Doug will you and your angel friends please move some of these cars out of the way." It's just a chuckle I have with myself . . . and with Doug if he's listening.

My sister's son who is the youngest cousin, went to the Iraq war. I asked Doug and his angel friends to be with him. I emailed my nephew while he was still in Iraq. He wrote back to me, "I constantly feel Doug's presence with me. I also carry Doug's social security card with me where ever I go."

We had no clue that he had Doug's social security card because we could never find it. My husband and I purposely looked for it, to put it with his other papers. Now we know why.

My son was very charismatic. He was a strapping big fellow and people gravitated to him. Curiously during the last two years of his life, he was intrigued by life-after-life movies. He'd call me, "Mom, have you seen 'Meet Joe Black' yet? Check it out."

GUEST STORY

I met Barbara Hobbs at a writing workshop in Chapel Hill. Out of two dozen people, she wound up sitting next to me. We began talking during the lunch break. This often happens that someone with a ghostly experience somehow unknowingly engages in a conversation with me. It's as if an unseen hand guides us until we meet so their story can be told. This is her story as she wrote it.

The Strange Visits of William King By Barbara H. Hobbs

Today my name is Barbara Hobbs, but in the late 1980s it was Barbara Battles. I lived on Versailles in Plano, Texas, a modest 3-bedroom home in a north Dallas suburb. There was a small cozy den on the west side of the house, which featured a fireplace that opened into the living room beyond as well. The fireplace was flanked by cabinets topped by shelves, which stopped at normal room height. However, since the ceilings were high in the room, there was a 2 foot opening above the top bookshelf. As part of my decorating, I had placed a basket of dried flowers there. The basket was not small - 24" x 10" x 8" with a handle in the middle. The arrangement was pretty large, and the basket filled most of the space above the shelf.

    One day (I don't remember the exact date but it would have been in the late 1980s) I came home from work to find the basket on the floor across the room near the door to the kitchen area. It was on its side as if thrown or as if it might have fallen. However, if the latter were true, the basket would have fallen down closer to the bookshelf, not across the room. My husband simply thought an animal had somehow run behind it and knocked it off. I don't find this plausible at all. For one thing, it would have taken a pretty sizeable animal to knock the basket off, and how would that animal gotten to the top of the bookshelf? Also, the basket would have been found closer to the bookshelf, not across the room.

The issue remained unresolved, and I thought nothing of it. However a couple of weeks later I noticed that the king on the chess set displayed on a side table was turned toward the room instead of into the board. The set was a decorative carved stone group set on a marble board. I thought it was odd but merely turned the piece around to its normal position without noting it to anyone. The next day the piece was turned again. Remembering the basket and not wanting the chess set damaged, I moved it to the living room where no further changes occurred.

By this time, I began to have the feeling that there was a presence of some sort in the room. I am not a big believer in the paranormal but allow the fact that some things cannot be explained by normal knowledge. I had a friend who *was* deeply into the paranormal. She and two of her group came over to sit in the room and see if they sensed anything. She brought a Ouija board with her and using it as a guide, came up with the name of William. We put it together with the name of the chess piece—King—to come up with our ghost's name.

I had a chair in the den where I sat to read. It sat next to the fireplace facing into the room. One evening as I was reading, I sensed a presence behind me. I turned to see a man dressed in a gold suit with white shirt and brown tie. He was a thin Caucasian man approximately 40 years old. He wore a hat, which I thought was odd. Sort of a '40s look. He made no effort to communicate and the image disappeared rather quickly. It was the only time I ever saw him.

We had bought the home in 1985 and were not the original owners. I believe that it was built in the early 1980s. I always wanted to check the police records in Plano to see if there had been a Missing Persons report on a man named William King. Possibly he had come to an untimely death and was buried under the den.

I am an educated Caucasian woman. I taught high school French for 22 years before becoming an Executive Assistant for some 20 years. I read voraciously but do not have an inordinate interest in the occult. I never read science fiction. While I found my friend's interest in the paranormal interesting, I did not take it very seriously. I am a religious woman but do not follow the belief in the presence of ancestors around us. I feel that I am a credible person whose integrity would not permit me to make up something like this. I simply submit the story as I experienced it along with my thought on a possible explanation.

Author's Note: I researched this name and found there was a man by the name of William E. King living in Dallas, Texas. He was born 3 November 1909 and passed away on 28 July of 1980. He may have had an emotional tie to Barbara's house or may have just been stumbling around trying to find his way from his earthly life to the after-life.

SOURCES

1. Civil War Generalships, The Art of Command –William J. Wood
2. North Carolina University Magazine Vol. 6-7
3. Sketches of Old Warrenton, North Carolina-Lizzie Wilson Montgomery
4. The County of Warren, North Carolina 1586-1917
5. The Architecture of Warren County, North Carolina 1770s-1860s
6. Blaylock Archives
7. From Southern Historical Collection; Collection Number: 00590
   Collection Title: Person Family Papers, 1728-1907
8. Braswell Genealogy
9. Town Leaders, Littleton, North Carolina 1790-1920-Rebecca Leach Dozier
10. Thomas Person, North Carolina Booklet, vol. IX, no. 1 Stephen B Weeks,
11. Dictionary of North Carolina Biography, V, -William S. Powell, ed.
12. North Carolina Preservation-Catherine Bishir
13. Marquis de Lafayette Collection of Cleveland State University
14. Revolutionary Patriots of Prince George's County, MD, 1775-1783 Henry C. Peden
15. Historical Register of Officers of the Continental Army-Francis Bernard Heitman

16. Biographical History of North Carolina- Colonial Times Vol 6 by Samuel A'Court Ashe
17. Samuel Peter Arrington Bible Record
18. Bible of Hannah Bolton White
19. Pitard Genealogy
20. American National Biography Online
21. The Star, December 26, 1838.
22. North Carolina Schools & Academies, 1790-1840, by Charles L. Coon 1914
23. Fauquier Times-Democrat newspaper, 15 April 1998 "Ghost on Falmouth Street" Joe Winkelmann.

Made in the USA
Charleston, SC
08 March 2016